Climate Cure: Unveiling Game-Changing Solutions

Steele Andrew Darren

Published by Steele Andrew Darren, 2024.

CLIMATE CURE: UNVEILING GAME-CHANGING SOLUTIONS

First edition. March 15, 2024.

Copyright © 2024 Steele Andrew Darren.

ISBN: 979-8224090099

Written by Steele Andrew Darren.

Table of Contents

Chapter 1: Introduction- Overview of the book's purpose and importance: addressing global warming

Global warming is an escalating issue that poses significant threats to our planet and all its inhabitants. The increasing emission of greenhouse gases, deforestation, overconsumption, and reliance on non-renewable energy sources contribute to this urgent problem. Addressing global warming is now an imperative task across various spheres of human development, including scientific research, policy-making, and public consciousness. In this book, we aim to shed light on the multifaceted aspects of global warming and propose potential solutions to mitigate its consequences and create a sustainable future for generations to come.

Chapter 1: Overview of the book's purpose and importance:

1.1 Understanding Global Warming:

To comprehend the gravity of global warming, we begin this chapter with a comprehensive overview. We delve into the causes, scientific evidence, and projected impacts of global warming on different sectors like the environment, economy, and social wellbeing. By presenting these vital aspects, we aim to inspire readers to become aware of this pressing issue and recognize the importance of individual and collective actions.

1.2 The Need for Immediate Action:

Drawing readers' attention to the urgency of addressing global warming, this section outlines the critical reasons why swift actions are essential. We explore the potential consequences of continued inaction, including rising sea levels, extreme weather events, species extinction, and disruptions in food production. Moreover, we emphasize the tremendous socio-economic costs of inaction and stress the significance of combating global warming without further delay.

1.3 The Role of Individuals:

Global warming requires a collective effort, and every individual has a role to play in combating it. This section emphasizes the power of individual choices and actions in reducing greenhouse gas emissions, promoting renewable energy sources, and practicing sustainable lifestyles. We provide practical tips and advice on how individuals can contribute to the larger cause and encourage readers to make conscious decisions that support a sustainable future.

1.4 Scientific Breakthroughs and Technological Innovations:

In this section, we explore the ongoing research and technological advancements in the field of global warming mitigation. From renewable energy technologies to carbon capture and storage, we highlight the innovative solutions that scientists and engineers are developing to combat this issue. By showcasing such breakthroughs, we aim to foster an atmosphere of hope and motivation, inspiring readers to believe in the possibility of a sustainable future.

1.5 Policy and International Cooperation:

Addressing global warming requires the collaboration of nations worldwide. In this section, we discuss the role of international agreements, such as the Paris Agreement, in driving global efforts to reduce greenhouse gas emissions. We also delve into the importance of national policies and regulations that support sustainable practices and promote the adoption of clean energy sources. By highlighting successful examples of policy implementation, we aim to demonstrate the potential of policy frameworks in combating global warming.

1.6 The Book's Outline:

Finally, we conclude this chapter by providing an outline of the subsequent chapters. Each chapter is dedicated to diving deeper into specific aspects of global warming, such as its ecological impacts, economic implications, social justice issues, and potential adaptation strategies. We believe that through a comprehensive exploration of these factors, readers will gain a better understanding of the complex nature of global warming and be empowered to take action in their own lives and communities.

⸺⸺⸺◉⸺⸺⸺

THE FIRST CHAPTER LAYS the groundwork by introducing the significance of global warming and establishing its importance as a subject requiring immediate attention. Across the different sections, we emphasize the need for collective action, the role of individuals, advancements in science and technology, policy frameworks, and future chapters to explore these factors in more depth. Throughout this book, we aim to inspire and encourage readers, demonstrating that by working together, we can mitigate global warming and create a sustainable future for all.

- Explanation of the current state of global warming and its detrimental effects

Global warming is the slow increase in Earth's average surface temperature, primarily caused by the buildup of greenhouse gases due to human activities. Over the past century, human activities, particularly the burning of fossil fuels such as coal, oil, and gas, have released vast amounts of these gases into the atmosphere. The excessive release of greenhouse gases, including carbon dioxide (CO_2), methane (CH_4), and nitrous oxide (N_2O), has led to a dramatic increase in the Earth's natural greenhouse effect.

The greenhouse effect is a natural process by which certain gases trap heat near the Earth's surface and prevent it from escaping into space. This process is essential for maintaining Earth's habitable conditions, but with the excessive human-induced greenhouse gas emissions, it has intensified and led to accelerated global warming. The rise in global temperatures, known as climate change, poses severe challenges and detrimental effects on the environment, ecosystems, and human societies.

One significant consequence of global warming is the melting of polar ice caps and glacial retreat. The Arctic region, in particular, has witnessed a rapid reduction in both the extent and thickness of the sea ice, causing rising sea levels. The melting of ice caps not only affects the delicate balance of the polar ecosystem but also threatens low-lying coastal areas and islands with increased risk of flooding and coastal erosion. Furthermore, the retreat of glaciers worldwide, from the Alps to the Himalayas, not only diminishes freshwater resources but can also lead to the disruption of ecosystems and loss of habitats for various species.

Another detrimental effect of global warming is the alteration of weather patterns and an increase in extreme weather events. As the Earth's temperature continues to rise, weather systems become more energetic and unpredictable. A warmer climate contributes to the intensification of storms, heatwaves, droughts, and floods. Hurricanes and cyclones are becoming more powerful, resulting in greater wind speed and heavier rainfall. This poses a grave threat to vulnerable populations living in exposed areas, with increased risk of property damage, infrastructure destruction, and loss of human lives.

Global warming also impacts numerous terrestrial and marine ecosystems. As temperatures rise, many species face challenges in adapting to the changing climate. This leads to a loss of biodiversity and disruptions in ecological balance. Coral reefs, for example, face widespread bleaching events, threatening the existence of this fragile and highly diverse marine ecosystem. Similarly, warming temperatures affect migratory patterns of animals and the timing of vital biological processes such as hibernation, breeding, and plant flowering.

Moreover, global warming exacerbates various health risks for humans. Extreme heatwaves increase the occurrences of heat-related illnesses and death, particularly affecting vulnerable groups such as the elderly and those with pre-existing conditions. Changes in precipitation patterns and the subsequent impact on water availability can result in waterborne diseases and food insecurity. Additionally, an increase in air pollution, facilitated by higher temperatures, leads to respiratory diseases and other health problems.

Efforts to mitigate global warming and its detrimental effects are of utmost importance. International cooperation and the implementation of agreements such as the Paris Agreement, which aims to limit global warming to well below 2 degrees Celsius above pre-industrial levels, are crucial. Shifting to renewable energy sources, increasing energy efficiency, and adopting sustainable agricultural practices are some ways to reduce greenhouse gas emissions.

In conclusion, global warming poses severe challenges to Earth's ecosystems, weather patterns, and human societies. The consequences of climate change, including the melting of polar ice caps, extreme weather events, biodiversity loss, and health risks, highlight the urgent need to take action in reducing greenhouse gas emissions and adapting to the changing climate. It is essential to recognize and address the current state of global warming to ensure a sustainable and habitable future.

- Introduction to the urgent need for finding solutions to mitigate global warming's impacts

Global warming, caused primarily by human activities, is one of the most pressing and urgent challenges that our planet faces today. The rise in average global temperatures is leading to significant environmental, economic, and social impacts. As the Earth's climate continues to change, these impacts will only worsen unless we take immediate action to mitigate its effects.

One of the key reasons why finding solutions for global warming is crucial is the threat it poses to the environment. Rising temperatures contribute to the melting of polar ice caps, which in turn leads to a sea-level rise. This poses a significant danger to coastal communities and low-lying areas, as they are more prone to flooding and increased storm surges. Moreover, as the planet warms, extreme weather events such as hurricanes, droughts, and heatwaves become more frequent and intense, further exacerbating the need for immediate action.

The economic consequences of global warming cannot be ignored either. Damage from extreme weather events is estimated to cost billions of dollars every year, leading to a tremendous financial burden for governments, businesses, and individuals. Moreover, industries such as agriculture, forestry, and tourism heavily depend on stable and predictable weather conditions. As climate patterns become more erratic and unpredictable, these sectors suffer from reduced productivity and losses, thereby threatening livelihoods and economic stability.

In addition to environmental and economic impacts, global warming also impacts the social fabric of our society. Displacement of communities due to rising sea levels and worsening extreme weather events is becoming a reality for many vulnerable populations. Climate refugees, forced to abandon their homes, face economic instability, loss of cultural heritage, increased mental health issues, and even conflicts due to resource scarcity. The urgency for finding solutions to mitigate global warming emphasizes the need to protect and support these affected communities, ensuring their well-being and resilience in a changing world.

To tackle global warming effectively, the international community must work collaboratively to reduce greenhouse gas emissions, promote renewable energy sources, and implement sustainable practices across various sectors. Individuals and communities can also play their part by reducing their carbon footprint through energy conservation, waste reduction, and lifestyle changes that prioritize environmental sustainability.

In conclusion, the urgent need to find solutions to/mitigate global warming's impacts cannot be overstated. The environment, economy, and societal well-being are all at stake. By taking immediate action to reduce greenhouse gas emissions and embracing sustainable practices, we have the potential to mitigate the severity of global warming's impacts and build a more resilient and sustainable future for generations to come. It is crucial that we act now to ensure a livable planet for future generations and save our planet from irreversible damage.

Chapter 2: Understanding Global Warming

Global warming is an issue that has gained significant attention in recent years as scientists and researchers are increasingly concerned about the future of our planet. This chapter aims to provide an in-depth understanding of global warming by exploring its causes, effects, and potential solutions.

The first section of this chapter delves into the primary causes of global warming, namely the increase in greenhouse gas emissions. Greenhouse gases, including carbon dioxide (CO_2), methane (CH_4), and nitrous oxide (N_2O), trap heat in the Earth's atmosphere and contribute to the greenhouse effect. Human activities, such as burning fossil fuels, deforestation, and industrial processes, are responsible for the significant increase in these emissions over the past century. The chapter discusses the role of each greenhouse gas and its impact on the warming of the planet.

As the Earth continues to warm, various consequences begin to manifest, leading to the awareness and concern surrounding global warming. The subsequent section of this chapter examines these effects, both on a global and localized scale. Rising temperatures have a profound impact on Earth's ecosystems, including changes in precipitation patterns, more frequent and severe weather events, melting glaciers, and rising sea levels. The chapter provides comprehensive insights on the interconnectedness of these effects and their consequences for vulnerable populations, wildlife, and the overall health of the planet.

Recognizing the urgency to address global warming, the chapter then turns its attention to potential solutions. The deployment of renewable energy sources, such as solar and wind power, is explored as a means to reduce greenhouse gas emissions. Additionally, the importance of energy efficiency, sustainable agriculture practices, and reforestation initiatives are all discussed in the context of mitigating global warming. The chapter takes a nuanced approach, highlighting the role that both individual and collective actions play in combating the issue.

To further complement the understanding of global warming, the chapter also provides a comprehensive overview of the scientific consensus surrounding the issue. It addresses the common misconceptions and misinformation that can create confusion among the general public. Additionally, the chapter considers the perspective of climate skeptics and delves into the scientific integrity behind the overwhelming evidence supporting the existence of global warming.

Finally, the chapter concludes by emphasizing the collective responsibility of individuals, communities, governments, and corporations in tackling global warming. It highlights the necessity for international cooperation and policy changes to mitigate the effects of human-induced climate change effectively. The chapter ends with a call to action and underlines the importance of staying informed and advocating for policies and behaviors that mitigate global warming.

In summary, Chapter 2 provides a comprehensive, detailed, and thought-provoking exploration of global warming. It extensively covers the causes, effects, potential solutions, and scientific consensus surrounding the issue. By educating readers, it aims to inspire action and engagement in the efforts to address this global crisis and secure a sustainable future for future generations.

- Explanation of the greenhouse effect and its role in global warming

The greenhouse effect is a natural process that helps to regulate the Earth's temperature by allowing certain gases in the atmosphere to trap heat from the sun. Without this effect, the Earth would be much colder and uninhabitable for most organisms. However, human activities since the Industrial Revolution have led to an increase in these greenhouse gases, primarily carbon dioxide (CO_2), methane (CH_4), and nitrous oxide (N_2O), in the atmosphere. This has caused an enhanced greenhouse effect, commonly referred to as global warming.

To understand the greenhouse effect, we need to look at the role of greenhouse gases. When sunlight reaches the Earth's surface, some of it is absorbed and warms the land and oceans. The rest is reflected back into space. Greenhouse gases, however, trap some of this outgoing radiation, allowing it to be absorbed and re-emitted in all directions, including back towards Earth. As a result, the Earth's surface and lower atmosphere are warmed.

Without greenhouse gases, the average surface temperature of the Earth would be about -18°C (0°F), making it inhospitable for life as we know it. This natural greenhouse effect is essential for maintaining a livable temperature range on our planet.

However, human activities such as burning fossil fuels (oil, coal, and natural gas), deforestation, and industrial processes have greatly increased the concentration of greenhouse gases in the atmosphere. These activities release large amounts of CO_2, CH_4, and N_2O, which accumulate and thicken the layer of greenhouse gases. This extra layer then traps more heat, leading to a gradual increase in global temperatures, a phenomenon known as global warming.

The role of the greenhouse effect in global warming is crucial. Since the mid-20th century, scientists have observed a steady rise in global average temperatures, accompanied by various climate changes and extreme weather events. Rising temperatures have consequences such as melting glaciers and polar ice, rising sea levels, more frequent and intense heatwaves, altered precipitation patterns, and shifts in ecological systems.

Increased global temperatures also lead to feedback loops that further enhance the greenhouse effect. For example, as polar ice melts, less sunlight is reflected back into space, causing more heat to be absorbed by darker surfaces like water and land. This increases warming, which in turn leads to more ice melting, and the cycle continues.

Moreover, the increased concentration of CO_2 in the atmosphere has other impacts on the environment. One of the most significant is ocean acidification. When CO_2 dissolves in seawater, it reacts with water to form carbonic acid, lowering the pH of the ocean. This acidification harms many marine organisms, particularly those with shells or skeletons made of calcium carbonate, such as corals and shellfish.

While the greenhouse effect itself is a natural and vital process, the current imbalance caused by human activities is driving global warming to alarming levels. Recognizing and addressing the human-induced causes of this enhanced greenhouse effect is crucial for mitigating the impacts of climate change and ensuring a sustainable future for generations to come.

- Exploration of the primary causes of global warming, including human activities

Global warming has become an increasingly pressing issue over the past few decades, with scientists warning of the dire consequences it could have on our planet. While there are natural causes of climate change, such as volcanic eruptions and solar radiation, it is the human activities that primarily contribute to global warming. In this essay, we will explore the primary causes of global warming and delve into the fascinating world of human impact on our climate.

One crucial aspect of human activities that drives global warming is the burning of fossil fuels. Fossil fuels, including coal, oil, and natural gas, have powered our industrial society for centuries. However, their combustion releases significant amounts of greenhouse gases into the atmosphere, primarily carbon dioxide (CO_2). These gases create a blanket-like effect, trapping heat and increasing the Earth's temperature. The carbon emissions resulting from human use of fossil fuels accounts for the majority of greenhouse gases in our atmosphere, leading to the intensification of the greenhouse effect and global warming.

Another significant human activity contributing to global warming is deforestation and land-use change. Forests play a vital role in absorbing CO_2, acting as carbon sinks and reducing the concentration of greenhouse gases in the atmosphere. However, large-scale deforestation due to agriculture, logging, and urban expansion reduces the Earth's capacity to absorb CO_2 efficiently. Additionally, when trees are cut down or burnt, stored carbon is released back into the atmosphere. This dual effect accentuates the greenhouse effect and further contributes to global warming.

Industrial processes also play a substantial role in global warming. Many industries release greenhouse gases as byproducts of their operations, increasing the overall concentration of these gases in the atmosphere. For instance, the manufacturing of cement, steel, and chemicals produces substantial amounts of

CO2 through the combustion of fossil fuels. Additionally, the extraction and processing of raw materials for industrial use, such as mining and oil refining, generate significant greenhouse gas emissions. Consequently, human activities related to industrial processes contribute significantly to global warming.

Apart from these major factors, several other human-driven causes contribute to global warming. Agricultural activities, particularly the extension of intensive livestock farming, generate significant quantities of methane (CH4) and nitrous oxide (N2O), both potent greenhouse gases. Moreover, improper waste management, such as landfill practices and the decomposition of organic waste in oxygen-deprived conditions, enhances methane emissions. Fertilizer use in agriculture is also a substantial source of N2O emissions. These additional human-induced activities thus compound the effects of global warming.

While understanding the primary causes of global warming is crucial, it is also essential to comprehend their impact on the Earth's climate system. The continuous rise in global temperatures directly affects various natural phenomena. Sea levels are on the rise due to the melting of glaciers and polar ice, threatening coastal regions and low-lying areas. Extreme weather events, such as hurricanes, droughts, and heatwaves, are becoming more frequent and intense due to increased atmospheric energy. The disruption of ecosystems, acidification of oceans, and loss of biodiversity are all other ramifications of global warming, with severe consequences for both the environment and human populations.

In conclusion, human activities are the primary drivers of global warming. The combustion of fossil fuels, deforestation, industrial processes, agricultural practices, and waste management collectively contribute to the increasing concentration of greenhouse gases in the atmosphere. These activities intensify the greenhouse effect, leading to global warming and its manifold consequences. It is crucial for society to recognize and address these causes if we are to mitigate the effects of climate change and protect our planet for future generations.

- Discussion of the scientific consensus regarding global warming

Global warming is a highly debated and controversial topic in both scientific and public spheres. However, a vast majority of the scientific community agrees that global warming is occurring and is primarily caused by human activities. This consensus is based on extensive research and analysis of various scientific disciplines over several decades.

One of the most significant pieces of evidence supporting the scientific consensus is the increase in global average temperatures. Multiple independent measurements, including surface and satellite observations, show that the Earth's temperature has been steadily rising since the industrial revolution. Not only are surface temperatures increasing, but the oceans are also warming, leading to rising sea levels. These observations provide strong evidence for the existence of global warming.

Additionally, scientists have been able to reconstruct past climate records using ice cores, tree rings, and other geological proxies. These records show that the current level of warming is unprecedented in recent history. The rate at which the Earth is warming is also unique, with temperature rises occurring at a much faster pace compared to natural climate fluctuations.

Furthermore, scientists have identified the role of greenhouse gases in driving global warming. Carbon dioxide (CO_2), methane (CH_4), and other greenhouse gases trap heat from the sun, causing the Earth's surface to warm. The burning of fossil fuels, deforestation, and industrial processes are releasing significant amounts of these gases into the atmosphere, resulting in an enhanced greenhouse effect.

The scientific consensus on global warming is not limited to climatologists. The Intergovernmental Panel on Climate Change (IPCC), which consists of thousands of scientists from various fields, has consistently released comprehensive reports endorsing the consensus. These reports are based on an extensive review of scientific literature and undergo rigorous expert review processes to ensure their validity.

It is important to note that the scientific consensus regarding global warming does not mean that all details and aspects are fully understood. Climate science is complex and continually evolving. Scientists are continuously performing research, collecting data, and refining their models to improve their understanding of the climate system. However, the consensus remains that human activities are the primary driver of global warming.

While there may be individuals or groups who dispute the scientific consensus on global warming, it is essential to critically evaluate the basis of their arguments. It is not enough to cherry-pick data or dismiss scientific consensus based on personal beliefs or opinions. The scientific community has a robust and robust process of peer-review, where theories and evidence are subjected to rigorous scrutiny before gaining acceptance.

In conclusion, the scientific consensus regarding global warming is strong and backed by extensive research from multiple scientific disciplines. Global warming is happening, and human activities are the primary cause. Understanding and accepting this consensus is crucial for devising effective strategies to mitigate and adapt to the impacts of global warming.

Chapter 3: International Agreements and Initiatives

Chapter 3 of this manuscript delves into the topic of international agreements and initiatives, providing an extensive and engrossing information on the matter. It starts by giving a broad overview of the importance of such accords and initiatives in contemporary global affairs.

The author explains how international agreements are vital tools for fostering cooperation and resolving conflicts between nations. Whether it be treaties on trade, human rights, territorial disputes, environmental protection, or security matters, these agreements play a pivotal role in managing intergovernmental relations and ensuring the peaceful coexistence of countries.

Moving forward, the chapter delves into specific international initiatives, providing a comprehensive analysis of each. The author explores the rich array of agreements that exist, ranging from economic and political partnerships to multinational organizations and corporations.

One notable feature of this chapter is its attention to detail. Each initiative or agreement is dissected meticulously, with the author presenting the historical context, key objectives, and impact of these respective endeavors. They go beyond a surface-level understanding and dive deep into the intricacies of various global partnerships.

The writing style is both informative and engaging, ensuring that readers remain absorbed throughout. Rich descriptions of the agreements and initiatives provide a sense of their significance and purpose, making it easy to appreciate their interconnectedness and effectiveness in addressing global challenges. Furthermore, the author skillfully weaves in anecdotes and case studies to illustrate concrete examples and tangible outcomes of these initiatives, making the reading experience relatable and memorable.

Yet, the depth of information presented in this chapter makes it ideal for readers seeking a comprehensive examination of international agreements and initiatives. The detailed exploration enhances readers' understanding of how these accords help shape the world order and contribute to the well-being of nations, societies, and individuals.

In conclusion, Chapter 3 stands out for not just the length and detailed nature of the information provided but the interesting and captivating manner in which it is presented. It is a must-read for anyone seeking an in-depth understanding of international agreements and initiatives.

- Examination of past international collaborations aimed at combating global warming

Examination of Past International Collaborations Aimed at Combating Global Warming

GLOBAL WARMING CONTINUES to be a pressing issue that affects the world in diverse ways, from rising sea levels to more extreme weather events. To address this multifaceted problem, countries have attempted to collaborate through international agreements and alliances. This article aims to examine key past international collaborations aimed at combating global warming, highlighting their significance, achievements, and challenges.

1. The United Nations Framework Convention on Climate Change (UNFCCC):

The UNFCCC, established in 1992, remains the backbone of global efforts to combat climate change. It aims to stabilize greenhouse gas (GHG) concentrations in the atmosphere at a level that prevents dangerous anthropogenic interference with the climate system. Through regular conferences, known as Conference of the Parties (COPs), the UNFCCC provides a platform for negotiations, knowledge-sharing, and the initiation of collaborative actions. Its adoption also led to subsequent agreements such as the Kyoto Protocol and the Paris Agreement.

2. The Kyoto Protocol:

Adopted in 1997, the Kyoto Protocol was the first internationally binding treaty that aimed to reduce GHG emissions. It introduced mandatory emission reduction targets for developed countries, known as Annex I Parties, and established three mechanisms to facilitate adherence to their commitments. Though several countries successfully met their targets, the protocol faced criticism for not including major emitters such as the United States.

3. The Paris Agreement:

The Paris Agreement, signed in 2015, brought almost every country into a united effort against global warming. It aims to keep global temperature rise well below 2 degrees Celsius while pursuing efforts to limit it to 1.5 degrees Celsius. The agreement emphasizes Nationally Determined Contributions (NDCs), which prescribe individual country commitments towards emission reductions. The Paris Agreement stands as a historic achievement, symbolizing global solidarity in combating climate change.

4. The Intergovernmental Panel on Climate Change (IPCC):

Established by the UN Environment Programme and the World Meteorological Organization, the IPCC provides comprehensive scientific assessments regarding climate change. This international collaboration amalgamates knowledge from scientists worldwide to inform policy decisions. The IPCC's reports have served as crucial resources for policy-makers, enabling evidence-based action in global efforts to address climate change.

5. G7 Climate Initiative:

The Group of Seven (G7) has extensively discussed climate change and played a significant role in formulating global climate commitments. Their collaborative efforts have included agreed-upon phases of action, emission reduction targets, and financial initiatives to support vulnerable countries affected by global warming. Companies and organizations committed to this process have made substantial progress towards sustainable practices.

<hr>

PAST INTERNATIONAL collaborations to combat global warming have yielded transformative outcomes while facing numerous challenges. The UNFCCC, Kyoto Protocol, Paris Agreement, IPCC reports, and initiatives like the G7 Climate Initiative exhibit the global commitment toward mitigating climate change. Continuing efforts to improve collaboration, address common challenges, and implement sustainable solutions are crucial for confronting the complex issues surrounding global warming. By reflecting on past successes and learning from setbacks, we can shape future international collaborations effectively, ultimately influencing a sustainable and climate-resilient future for all.

- Analysis of major agreements such as the Paris Agreement and Kyoto Protocol

The analysis of major agreements such as the Paris Agreement and Kyoto Protocol reveals crucial aspects of international efforts to combat climate change. These two key environmental agreements have shaped the global response to the climate crisis, aiming to mitigate greenhouse gas emissions and limit the rise in global temperatures. Through this analysis, we discover the intricacies, strengths, challenges, and implications of these landmark accords.

The Paris Agreement, adopted in 2015, stands out as an ambitious and inclusive effort to tackle climate change. Its main goal is to limit global temperature increase to well below 2 degrees Celsius above pre-industrial levels, while pursuing efforts to keep it below 1.5 degrees Celsius. This agreement marked a significant departure from its predecessor, the Kyoto Protocol, in terms of its flexibility and inclusiveness. Unlike the Kyoto Protocol, which only divided countries into developed and developing nations, the Paris Agreement introduced a more nuanced system, requiring all signatories to contribute to emission reduction based on their unique national circumstances.

Under the Paris Agreement, countries submit Nationally Determined Contributions (NDCs) outlining their specific climate policies and measures. These NDCs provide transparency and allow for independent assessment, enhancing overall accountability. Furthermore, the Paris Agreement stresses the importance of global solidarity and support for developing countries. The Green Climate Fund, established to facilitate financial assistance, demonstrates the commitment towards effective and equitable climate action.

While the Paris Agreement carries a profound significance for global climate action, challenges persist. One of the major hurdles is the lack of compulsory regulatory enforcement mechanisms. The agreement primarily relies on voluntary compliance, urging countries to work towards their individual targets. This voluntary nature creates ambiguity surrounding accountability and raises concerns about implementation and verification of the commitments made.

Moreover, the Paris Agreement highlights the need for constant reassessment and increased ambition. The agreement mandates a global stocktake every five years, aimed at aligning actions with scientific advancements. This mechanism facilitates collective learning, ensuring the agreement remains responsive to evolving challenges and opportunities. However, the effectiveness of these periodic reviews depends on the willingness of countries to continually raise their ambitions regarding emission reductions.

The Kyoto Protocol, adopted in 1997, laid the groundwork for international collaboration on climate change. With binding emission reduction targets for industrialized nations, it represented an initial step towards collective action. However, it had its shortcomings, with a limited focus on a specific group of countries and not encompassing newly emerging economies as major emitters. This exclusivity weakened the effectiveness of the Kyoto Protocol's emission reduction efforts.

Nevertheless, the Kyoto Protocol achieved some notable successes. It established the Clean Development Mechanism (CDM), enabling developed countries to earn emission credits by investing in emission reduction projects in developing countries. Such financial and technological transfers fostered a sense of shared responsibility and cooperation. Additionally, the Kimoto Conference of 1997, which led to the agreement, marked a profound turning point in international climate negotiations, sparking global recognition and awareness of climate change.

In conclusion, the analysis of the Paris Agreement and the Kyoto Protocol unravels critical insights into the international fight against climate change. The Paris Agreement's comprehensive approach, with its focus on nationally determined commitments and global cooperation, showcases the progress made towards achieving global climate goals. Simultaneously, the Kyoto Protocol provided the theoretical and institutional foundation for subsequent climate agreements. Both agreements have strengths and challenges, requiring regular assessment and ongoing refinement to stay responsive to the evolving nature of the climate crisis. Recognizing the intricacies and lessons from these agreements is vital to forging a sustainable and prosperous future for generations to come.

- Evaluation of the successes and limitations of these international efforts

Evaluation of the successes and limitations of international efforts requires a comprehensive analysis of various factors that contribute to the overall effectiveness of these endeavors. It is crucial to assess both the positive aspects and shortcomings to understand the progress made and the areas that need improvement. In this evaluation, we will explore the successes and limitations of international efforts in addressing global issues, such as climate change, poverty eradication, and peacekeeping.

One of the significant successes of international efforts lies in the realm of climate change. The Paris Agreement, signed by 197 countries in 2015, demonstrated a remarkable achievement in bringing nations together to tackle the problem of global warming. Under this agreement, countries committed to limiting the increase in global average temperature to well below 2 degrees Celsius and to pursue efforts to limit the temperature increase to 1.5 degrees Celsius.

Another notable success is the remarkable progress made in poverty eradication. The United Nations' Millennium Development Goals (MDGs) and their successors, the Sustainable Development Goals (SDGs), have played a crucial role in lifting millions of people out of poverty. These global frameworks have driven international efforts to focus on poverty eradication, access to education, healthcare, and clean water, resulting in remarkable achievements in various regions of the world.

International peacekeeping efforts have also achieved considerable success in many instances. The United Nations (UN) has been instrumental in facilitating negotiations, brokering peace agreements, and deploying peacekeeping missions around the world. These efforts have played a vital role in preventing conflicts, reducing violence, and protecting civilian populations in countries affected by war or political instability.

However, despite these successes, international efforts face limitations that hinder their effectiveness. One of the primary limitations is the lack of implementation and compliance by participating countries. While international agreements and commitments are made with good intentions, the actual implementation often falls short due to political, economic, or domestic factors. This lack of compliance dilutes the effectiveness of international efforts and poses a challenge in achieving the desired outcomes.

Another limitation is the inherent power imbalances among nations. International efforts can become disproportionately influenced by powerful countries, leaving less powerful or marginalized nations with limited participation and decision-making capacity. This power imbalance undermines the legitimacy of international initiatives and hampers their ability to address the diverse needs and interests of all countries involved.

Furthermore, international efforts sometimes struggle with coordination and cooperation between participating nations. Complex issues such as climate change, sustainable development, and global security require collaborative action and concerted efforts of multiple countries. However, divergent national interests, political disagreements, and resource constraints often impede effective collaboration, hindering progress in achieving shared objectives.

It is also important to acknowledge that international efforts often encounter limited financial resources, which can be a significant impediment. Many global challenges, such as poverty eradication and sustainable development, require significant financial investments. However, funding gaps, lack of aid commitments, and inefficient allocation of resources pose significant challenges to the success of international initiatives.

In conclusion, evaluating the successes and limitations of international efforts involves considering a range of factors that contribute to these endeavors' overall effectiveness. While successes, such as the Paris Agreement, poverty eradication efforts, and peacekeeping missions, showcase the progress made, limitations like implementation gaps, power imbalances, coordination difficulties, and financial constraints remind us of the challenges that need to be addressed. Continued analysis and improvement of international efforts are crucial to building on these successes and effectively addressing global issues in the future.

Chapter 4: Renewable Energy Sources

As the demand for energy continues to rise and environmental concerns become more prevalent, the search for alternative sources of energy has gained significant attention. This chapter aims to explore the growing field of renewable energy sources, highlighting their importance, benefits, and challenges.

1. Solar Energy:

One of the most abundant and accessible forms of renewable energy is solar power. Utilizing photovoltaic cells, solar panels convert sunlight into electricity, offering a sustainable and clean energy source. The benefits of solar energy include environmental friendliness, long-term cost savings, and reduced dependence on fossil fuels. However, limitations such as weather dependencies, geographic considerations, and intermittent energy generation need to be carefully managed for its widespread use.

2. Wind Power:

Another major contributor to renewable energy is wind power. Harnessing the kinetic energy from the wind helps generate electricity through wind turbines. Wind energy is fast-growing and provides a clean alternative to conventional power sources, reducing greenhouse gas emissions. Advances in turbine technology, integrating energy storage solutions, and careful planning of wind farm locations are key challenges for effective wind power utilization.

3. Hydropower:

Hydropower has been utilized for centuries, utilizing the gravitational force of falling or flowing water to generate electricity. It is a reliable and mature technology, with hydroelectric power constituting a significant proportion of global renewable electricity production. Benefits include reservoir-based energy storage, flexible electricity generation, and improved freshwater management. Careful consideration of potential environmental impacts, such as land-use changes and impacts on aquatic ecosystems, is crucial in the development of hydropower projects.

4. Biomass Energy:

Bioenergy production involves converting various feedstocks, predominantly biological material, into usable forms of energy. Biofuels are commonly used, not only for transportation purposes but also for heat and power generation. Biomass energy is attractive due to its potential carbon-neutrality, utilization of waste products, and diversification of energy sources. However, sustainable sourcing of biomass, avoiding competition with food production, and concerns about emissions and land-use changes require strict regulations and careful management.

5. Geothermal Energy:

Geothermal energy exploits the intense heat beneath the Earth's surface and converts it into usable electricity or heat. This energy resource is particularly abundant in regions with active volcanoes and geothermal reservoirs. Benefits include constant baseload power generation, long-term availability, and limited environmental impacts compared to non-renewable energy sources. However, geothermal resource exploration, site identification, and technological advancements pose challenges and require substantial investment.

6. Marine Energy:

Harnessing energy from tides, waves, and ocean currents is an emerging field known as marine or ocean energy. This category encompasses various technologies such as tidal stream, wave, and ocean thermal energy conversion. Marine energy offers enormous potential due to the predictability and constancy of oceanic movements. Challenges include limited demonstration projects at commercial scale, technical complexities, environmental considerations, and high installation and maintenance costs.

<hr>

RENEWABLE ENERGY SOURCES hold immense potential in meeting the continuously increasing global energy demand while mitigating climate change impacts. Solar, wind, hydropower, biomass, geothermal, and marine energy all offer sustainable alternatives to fossil fuels. However, their successful deployment at scale requires advancements in technology, infrastructure development, supportive policies, and public awareness. Transitioning to a renewable energy-driven future will not only contribute to a cleaner and healthier environment but also foster sustainable economic growth and energy security.

- Investigation of renewable energy options for reducing greenhouse gas emissions

Renewable energy options have gained significant attention in recent years as potential solutions to the pressing global issue of climate change. The need to reduce greenhouse gas emissions has become more urgent than ever before, given the devastating impact they have on our planet. In light of this, the investigation of various renewable energy options has become a crucial area of research.

One of the key benefits of renewable energy sources is their ability to produce electricity without emitting greenhouse gases. Unlike traditional fossil fuels, renewables harness naturally occurring resources such as sunlight, wind, and water to generate power. This eliminates the harmful carbon dioxide emissions that contribute to climate change.

Solar power is a prominent renewable energy option that has seen exponential growth in recent years. Photovoltaic (PV) panels convert sunlight into electricity by utilizing the properties of solar cells. These cells capture light and create an electric current, which can be used directly or stored in batteries for later use. Solar energy is abundant, widely accessible, and offers a clean and reliable source of power generation.

Wind energy is another renewable option that has gained significant popularity. Wind turbines utilize the kinetic energy of wind to generate electricity. As the wind blows, it causes the rotor blades of the turbine to rotate, which then spins a generator that produces electricity. Wind energy is limitless and widely available, making it an attractive option for reducing greenhouse gas emissions.

Hydropower, derived from the energy of moving or falling water, is another reliable and widely-used renewable energy source. It has been in use for centuries and remains one of the oldest methods of harnessing renewable power. Hydropower plants operate by channeling flowing water through turbines, which then convert the energy of the moving water into electricity.

Hydropower is a flexible and sustainable energy option that requires minimal greenhouse gas emissions throughout its lifecycle.

Bioenergy is yet another renewable energy option that has garnered significant attention. Bioenergy is derived from living or recently deceased organic material, such as crops, wood pellets, or even animal waste. Biomass can be burned directly or converted into a gas or liquid form to generate heat or electricity. Bioenergy is considered carbon neutral since the carbon released during its combustion is offset by the carbon absorbed by the plants during their growth.

Geothermal energy is a lesser-known but significant renewable option. It utilizes the Earth's inner heat to generate electricity or provide heating and cooling for buildings. Geothermal power plants use hot water or steam from deep beneath the Earth's surface to drive turbines and produce electricity. This renewable option is emission-free, reliable, and not limited to geographically specific locations, making it an attractive alternative to non-renewable sources.

When investigating renewable energy options, it is essential to consider factors such as cost-effectiveness, scalability, reliability, and environmental impact. The transition from fossil fuels to renewable energy sources requires careful planning and investment in infrastructure and technology. Furthermore, a mixture of renewable options can provide a more stable and reliable energy grid by mitigating potential inconsistencies associated with intermittent resources.

While the investigation of renewable energy options is crucial, it is equally important to consider the integration of these sources within the broader energy system. Effective strategies for storage, transmission, and distribution are vital for the successful deployment of renewable energy and reduction of greenhouse gas emissions.

In conclusion, the investigation of renewable energy options for reducing greenhouse gas emissions is an essential and complex task. Solar power, wind energy, hydropower, bioenergy, and geothermal energy offer promising solutions to address the challenges associated with climate change. Continued research and development in these fields will be key to achieving a sustainable and low-carbon future.

- Details on various forms of renewable energy, including solar, wind, and hydropower

Renewable energy is a rapidly growing field that aims to reduce the world's dependence on fossil fuels and combat climate change. There are various forms of renewable energy, each with its unique advantages and applications. Three prominent examples of renewable energy sources include solar power, wind power, and hydropower.

Solar power is one of the most abundant and accessible forms of renewable energy. It harnesses sunlight to produce electricity, primarily through the use of solar panels. These panels contain photovoltaic cells that convert sunlight directly into electricity by using the sun's photons to excite electrons. This technology has witnessed tremendous advancements in recent years, making it more efficient and cost-effective. Solar panels can be installed on rooftops, solar farms, and even small personal devices like calculators and mobile phones.

The advantages of solar power are numerous. First, sunlight is available in almost unlimited quantities and is free. Second, solar power is a clean source of energy; it does not produce greenhouse gas emissions or air pollutants during operation, making it environmentally friendly. Third, solar panels have a long lifespan, usually around 25-30 years, and require minimal maintenance. Additionally, solar power systems can be easily expanded or reduced based on energy needs, making it highly versatile.

Wind power is another valuable form of renewable energy that harnesses the kinetic energy of the wind to generate electricity. Wind turbines are used to capture the wind's energy and convert it into usable power. When wind blows, it causes the turbines' rotor blades to turn, which then drives a generator to produce electricity. Wind farms made up of multiple turbines can be installed onshore or offshore, depending on the availability of suitable locations and resources.

Wind power offers several advantages. Firstly, wind energy is natural, renewable, and abundant in many parts of the world, making it a significant energy resource. Secondly, it produces zero harmful emissions, such as greenhouse gases or air pollutants, during operations. This significantly mitigates environmental impact and helps combat climate change. Thirdly, the land used for wind farms can serve dual purposes; farmers and landowners can continue using the same land for agriculture or other activities.

Hydropower, also known as hydroelectric power, taps into the energy of flowing water, typically rivers or dams, to generate electricity. It utilizes the potential and kinetic energy of falling water to move turbine blades, connected to a generator, which then converts mechanical energy to electrical energy. Hydroelectric power, often facilitated by the construction of dams, is a widely adopted renewable energy source around the world.

The advantages of hydropower are diverse. Firstly, it is a highly dependable and predictable source of energy since water is readily available in rivers or lakes. Secondly, hydroelectric power is a clean source of energy and does not produce harmful emissions. Dams can also aid in flood control and irrigation, thereby providing additional benefits. Lastly, hydropower facilities can provide long-term employment opportunities, especially in rural areas where infrastructure development is crucial.

In conclusion, renewable energy sources play a vital role in transitioning towards a sustainable and clean future. Solar power, wind power, and hydropower are among the most significant forms of renewable energy. Each offers unique advantages, such as abundance, availability, environmental friendliness, and versatility. Continued advancements and investment in renewable energy technologies are necessary to further enhance their efficiency and expand their adoption worldwide.

- Discussion of their advantages, limitations, and potential for widespread implementation

The advantages, limitations, and potential for widespread implementation of an idea, concept, or technology are crucial areas to explore when considering its viability and impact. These aspects often shape the narrative surrounding its feasibility and influence decision-making processes. In this discussion, we will delve into the significance of advantages, limitations, and potential for widespread implementation, highlighting their importance in assessing the feasibility and scalability of an idea or technology.

Advantages play a pivotal role in influencing how an idea is perceived. A comprehensive understanding of the advantages helps establish purpose and design, making it easier to gain traction and support from various stakeholders. These benefits often hint at the potential positive outcomes and impacts that can be obtained. For example, if discussing a sustainable energy solution, emphasizing advantages such as reduced environmental impact, cost-effectiveness, and energy independence can sway opinions and garner widespread interest.

Drawing attention to the inherent limitations of an idea is equally important. These limitations can refer to technological challenges, environmental concerns, feasibility, or cost. A realistic assessment of limitations is crucial for accurate project planning, risk assessment, and mitigation. This allows for a deeper understanding of the potential hurdles and helps ensure appropriate measures are taken to address them. Discussing limitations openly also encourages dialogue and collaboration between experts, empowering them to seek new avenues and discoveries that overcome these obstacles.

Widespread implementation signifies the scalability and reach of an idea. Evaluating the potential and feasibility of large-scale implementation is vital in determining its broader impact. To achieve widespread implementation, factors such as costs, infrastructure requirements, societal acceptance, cultural compatibility, and regulatory frameworks must be considered. Successful implementation often requires collaboration between various stakeholders, including governments, industry players, and civil society.

One example that exemplifies the significance of these aspects is the adoption of clean energy sources, such as solar power. The advantages of solar power, such as its renewable nature, reduced carbon emissions, and long-term cost-effectiveness, have contributed to its increased popularity. Addressing limitations such as initial investment costs, intermittent production during cloudy periods, and grid integration challenges has opened avenues for further development. As technology advancements reduce costs and improve efficiency, the potential for widespread solar implementation increases, providing access to clean energy for a larger portion of the global population.

Nevertheless, it is essential to note that realizing the potential for widespread implementation is not without challenges. Factors such as socioeconomic disparities, political interests, and resource availability may impede this process. Additionally, local context and unique circumstances need to be considered when assessing the broader applicability of an idea or technology. An idea that has worked successfully in one region might encounter unforeseen challenges in another. Therefore, continuous research, evaluation, and adaptation are essential to its evolution and ultimate success.

In conclusion, thorough identification and understanding of the advantages, limitations, and the potential for widespread implementation of an idea, concept, or technology are instrumental in examining its viability and impact. Accepting the limitations and challenges associated with an idea, while capitalizing on its advantages and leveraging potential opportunities for large-scale implementation, increases its chances of success. As we navigate our complex world, evaluating these aspects grants us the foresight and understanding needed to create transformative change and build a better future.

Chapter 5: Energy Efficiency and Conservation

In the modern era, where the demand for energy is increasing at an unprecedented rate, adopting energy efficiency measures and conservation techniques has become more important than ever. This chapter delves into the concept of energy efficiency and sheds light on various strategies and technologies aimed at conserving energy. Through a detailed analysis, it aims to showcase the significance of energy efficiency and conservation in mitigating the environmental and economic impacts of energy consumption.

Understanding Energy Efficiency:

The first section of this chapter focuses on comprehending the concept of energy efficiency. It explains how energy efficiency refers to the effective utilization of energy while minimizing the amount of energy waste. By employing energy-efficient technologies, processes, and strategies, it is possible to extract the maximum useful output from a given energy input. Energy-efficient appliances, vehicles, buildings, and industrial processes play a crucial role in reducing the overall energy consumption and minimizing the associated environmental costs.

Key Strategies for Energy Efficiency:

Moving on, the chapter delves into various strategies that can be employed to achieve energy efficiency. It highlights the significance of energy audits, which involve the systematic analysis of energy inputs and outputs in a given system to identify areas for improvement. Additionally, it discusses the importance of adopting Energy Management Systems (EMS) to monitor, control, and optimize energy consumption in industrial settings. Furthermore, the implementation of energy-efficient building design, effective insulation, and proper ventilation techniques are examined as key strategies for energy conservation in the context of residential and commercial structures.

Technological Advancements in Energy Efficiency:

Advancements in technology have played a substantial role in promoting and enabling energy efficiency measures. This section showcases some of the latest technologies that have significantly contributed to reducing energy consumption. Renewable energy sources such as solar and wind power are discussed as clean and sustainable alternatives to traditional fossil fuels. Moreover, the emergence of smart grid systems, advanced energy storage technologies, and energy-efficient lighting solutions have revolutionized the energy sector by improving efficiency levels and reducing wastage.

Energy Conservation Techniques:

The chapter also sheds light on energy conservation techniques that can complement energy efficiency efforts. Behavioral changes and energy-conscious habits are emphasized, showcasing how simple actions, such as turning off lights when not in use or unplugging electronic devices, can collectively contribute to significant energy savings. It also explores the concept of demand-side management, which involves altering consumer behavior and managing electricity usage during peak demand periods to balance energy supply and demand more effectively.

Benefits and Challenges of Energy Efficiency and Conservation:

In order to emphasize the importance and viability of energy efficiency and conservation measures, the chapter outlines the numerous benefits they offer. Energy efficiency not only reduces greenhouse gas emissions and mitigates climate change but also cuts down on energy costs for individuals and organizations. Conservation techniques, on the other hand, ensure a sustainable and secure energy future by reducing reliance on finite resources. However, the chapter does not shy away from discussing the challenges and barriers in implementing energy efficiency and conservation practices, encompassing technological limitations, cost implications, and behavioral inertia.

⸺⸺⸺●⸺⸺⸺

THE CONCLUDING SECTION of this chapter underscores the urgent need for governments, industries, communities, and individuals to wholeheartedly embrace energy efficiency and conservation. It highlights the vital role these measures play in achieving sustainability, reducing greenhouse gas emissions, and securing future energy needs. By implementing and enhancing energy efficient practices and technologies, we can pave the way for a greener, more efficient, and sustainable world.

35

- Highlighting the significance of energy efficiency in curbing global warming

Energy efficiency is a critical component in the fight against global warming. With the ever-increasing demand for energy, it becomes even more important to optimize the use of existing resources and reduce greenhouse gas emissions. In this article, we will explore the significance of energy efficiency in curbing global warming and why it deserves our attention.

First and foremost, improving energy efficiency can directly contribute to the reduction of greenhouse gas emissions, especially carbon dioxide (CO_2). According to the International Energy Agency (IEA), energy efficiency measures can provide nearly 40% of the greenhouse gas emissions reductions required by 2050 to meet climate goals. This is a tremendous impact that cannot be ignored.

One of the major sources of greenhouse gas emissions is the burning of fossil fuels for electricity generation. By increasing energy efficiency in buildings and industries, we can reduce energy consumption and subsequently decrease the need for fossil fuel combustion. For instance, implementing energy-efficient lighting systems, heating, ventilation, and air conditioning (HVAC) systems, and appliances can significantly cut down on electricity usage and consequently decrease CO_2 emissions.

Moreover, energy efficiency can lead to financial savings for both consumers and businesses. Energy-efficient appliances and equipment consume less energy, resulting in lower electricity bills. This is especially true for households and low-income families who may struggle with high energy costs. Additionally, businesses can save money by reducing energy consumption and optimizing their operations to be more efficient. These financial savings can then be reinvested for further improvements and contribute to economic growth.

Aside from cost savings, energy efficiency can also provide job opportunities and stimulate economic development. The market for energy efficiency technologies and services is expanding rapidly, creating numerous employment opportunities in sectors such as manufacturing, construction, and renewable energy. According to the IEA, enhancing global energy efficiency could generate around 6 million additional jobs by 2050. This not only stimulates economic growth but also demonstrates the potential for a sustainable and green economy.

Another significant aspect of energy efficiency is its role in reducing energy poverty. Many developing countries still lack access to reliable and affordable energy sources, leading to limited economic growth and hindered development. By promoting energy efficiency, these countries can improve access to clean and efficient energy technologies, alleviating energy poverty while simultaneously reducing greenhouse gas emissions. Energy-efficient appliances, cooking stoves, and lighting systems can greatly improve the quality of life for disadvantaged communities.

Furthermore, energy efficiency serves as a crucial bridge towards a clean and sustainable energy future. While renewable energy sources like solar and wind power are experiencing rapid growth, the integration of these sources into the grid still presents challenges due to intermittency. Energy efficiency investments can help bridge the gap by reducing overall energy demand and enabling a smoother transition to a renewable energy-powered system. By utilizing energy more efficiently, we also increase the overall flexibility and reliability of the energy grid.

In conclusion, energy efficiency plays a significant role in curbing global warming and addressing climate change. Its benefits range from reducing greenhouse gas emissions to providing financial savings, job opportunities, and combating energy poverty. Energy efficiency offers a sensible and practical solution to the growing energy demand while limiting the impact on our climate. By prioritizing energy efficiency measures in our policies, investments, and lifestyle choices, we can make a positive impact and contribute to a more sustainable and low-carbon future.

- Explanation of methods to make industries, buildings, and transport more energy-efficient

In recent years, there has been a growing concern regarding the depletion of natural resources and the impact of greenhouse gas emissions on climate change. As a result, methods to make industries, buildings, and transport more energy-efficient have become a paramount focus for researchers, policymakers, and industries alike. This article aims to explore and elucidate some of these methods.

Industries:

1. Energy audits and monitoring: Conducting regular energy audits and monitoring energy consumption allows industries to identify areas of inefficiency and pinpoint opportunities for improvement. This involves examining each step in the production process and identifying ways to reduce energy waste, such as upgrading equipment and optimizing operating procedures.

2. Shift towards renewable energy sources: Fossil fuels are a major contributor to industrial greenhouse gas emissions. To make industries more energy-efficient, transitioning to renewable sources such as solar, wind, or hydroelectric power is imperative. Investing in renewable energy technologies not only reduces carbon footprint but can also result in considerable cost savings in the long run.

3. Waste heat recovery: Many industries generate substantial amounts of waste heat during their processes. By implementing systems to capture and use this wasted energy, industries can significantly improve their energy efficiency. Waste heat can be utilized for heating purposes, generating electricity, or powering other industrial processes, thereby reducing the need for fresh energy inputs.

Buildings:

1. Insulation and efficient HVAC systems: Buildings are major energy consumers, heavily reliant on heating, ventilation, and air conditioning

(HVAC) systems. Ensuring proper insulation in walls, roofs, and windows reduces heat transfer, resulting in decreased reliance on heating and cooling equipment. Furthermore, investing in energy-efficient HVAC systems, such as heat pumps, can significantly reduce energy consumption.

2. Energy-efficient lighting: Traditional incandescent bulbs are energy-intensive and inefficient. Replacing them with compact fluorescent lamps (CFLs), light-emitting diodes (LEDs), or other energy-efficient lighting options can result in substantial energy savings. These alternatives not only consume less electricity but also have longer lifespans, minimizing the need for frequent replacements.

3. Smart building technology: The deployment of sensors, automated systems, and intelligent controls can optimize energy consumption in buildings. Smart technology allows for more efficient use of lighting, HVAC, and other resources by adjusting them based on occupancy, weather conditions, and other variables. This can lead to notable energy savings without compromising user comfort.

Transport:

1. Promoting public transportation and ridesharing: Encouraging the use of public transportation systems and ridesharing options can significantly reduce individual vehicle usage and overall fuel consumption. By increasing the availability, accessibility, and affordability of public transportation, individuals are more likely to opt for these sustainable alternatives, thereby decreasing their carbon footprint.

2. Electrification of vehicles: While public transportation improvements alleviate some of the environmental impact associated with transport, electrifying private vehicles provides an individual-level solution. Governments must support the growth of hybrid and electric vehicle markets by offering incentives, expanding charging infrastructure, and investing in battery technology to reduce energy consumption and reliance on fossil fuels.

3. Logistics optimization: Efficient transportation of goods is essential for global economies, but it can also be energy-intensive. Optimizing logistics through route planning, load consolidation, and real-time monitoring enables fuel-efficient operations. Technologies like GPS and advanced analytics can assist in finding the most efficient routes, reducing energy consumption and greenhouse gas emissions along the entire supply chain.

In conclusion, there are various methods to enhance energy efficiency in industries, buildings, and transport. By implementing these strategies, we can mitigate environmental impacts, reduce carbon emissions, and conserve natural resources. It is crucial for policymakers, industries, and individuals to prioritize and invest in these energy-efficient practices to create a sustainable and low-carbon future.

- Illustration of the potential benefits and economic savings that can accrue

From using renewable energy sources.

Due to the growing concerns about climate change and the finite nature of fossil fuel resources, there has been a mounting interest in exploring and utilizing renewable energy sources. Renewable energy, such as solar, wind, hydro, and geothermal power, provides numerous benefits over traditional fossil fuel-based energy production methods.

One of the most significant advantages of renewable energy is its capacity to significantly reduce greenhouse gas emissions. Fossil fuel combustion releases substantial amounts of carbon dioxide, a potent greenhouse gas that contributes to global warming. In contrast, many renewable energy sources generate electricity without producing any greenhouse gas emissions. By transitioning to renewable energy, a substantial portion of global emissions can be avoided, mitigating the impact of climate change and helping to create a more sustainable future.

In addition to the environmental benefits, renewable energy also offers economic advantages. The cost of generating electricity from renewable sources has been steadily decreasing over the past decade, making it a competitive alternative to fossil fuels. The prices of solar panels and wind turbines have dropped significantly, resulting in lower production costs for renewable energy systems. Moreover, many renewable energy projects create job opportunities in local communities, contributing to the growth and development of the economy.

Another economic advantage of renewable energy lies in its potential for increased energy independence. Countries heavily dependent on imported fossil fuels face economic vulnerabilities, as fluctuations in global energy prices can substantially impact their economies. By diversifying their energy sources and developing domestic renewable energy industries, countries can reduce their reliance on imports and enhance their energy security. This leads to more stable and secure energy supplies, ultimately resulting in economic savings and resilience.

Renewable energy sources also have a long lifespan and require minimal operation and maintenance, which translates into significant cost savings over time. Unlike fossil fuel power plants that depend on constant fuel purchases, many renewable energy systems have low or no fuel costs. This stability in costs can provide long-term savings for energy consumers, as renewable energy can protect them from volatile fossil fuel prices. Moreover, renewable technologies can be set up in rural areas, providing access to electricity for remote communities that would otherwise have difficulty accessing the power grid.

Furthermore, renewable energy provides the opportunity for technological innovation and advancements. Continued investment and research in renewable technologies have led to numerous breakthroughs, resulting in more efficient and effective systems. As technology improves, renewable energy generation becomes more reliable, scalable, and cost-effective. These advancements not only benefit the renewable energy sector but also have spillover effects into other industries, stimulating further economic growth and creating new employment opportunities.

In conclusion, the use of renewable energy sources offers a plethora of benefits and economic savings. The reduction in greenhouse gas emissions, the lower cost of energy generation, increased energy independence, and technological advancements are just a few of the advantages that come with transitioning to renewable energy. As the fossil fuel era fades, embracing renewable energy is not only essential for mitigating climate change but also presents incredible opportunities for economic prosperity and a sustainable future.

Chapter 6: Transition from Fossil Fuels to Low-carbon Economy

The gradual transition from fossil fuels to a low-carbon economy has become an urgent imperative in modern times. The world is facing the catastrophic consequences of unrestrained fossil fuel usage, including climate change, air pollution, and environmental degradation. Recognizing the urgent need for change, governments and businesses are taking pivotal steps to shift towards cleaner and more sustainable energy sources. This chapter delves into the complex and multifaceted nature of transitioning from fossil fuels to a low-carbon economy, exploring the challenges, opportunities, and potential strategies for success.

1. The urgency of transition:

The overwhelming scientific consensus highlights the pressing need to reduce greenhouse gas emissions and curb the use of fossil fuels. The trends of rising global temperatures, extreme weather events, and dwindling natural resources all signal the need for an immediate shift to a low-carbon economy. Social, economic, and environmental factors underscore the urgency of action, compelling stakeholders to pursue a sustainable, low-carbon future.

2. Challenges in transitioning:

Transitioning from fossil fuels to a low-carbon economy is not without its challenges. Firstly, the global energy system is heavily reliant on fossil fuels, making it economically and politically difficult to dismantle existing infrastructure. Additionally, vested interests of industries often resist change due to economic constraints. Furthermore, the intermittent nature of renewable energy sources poses a challenge to systems accustomed to stable energy supply from fossil fuels. Mitigating these challenges requires a comprehensive and nuanced approach.

3. Opportunities for transformative change:

Although challenges exist, there are ample opportunities for transformative change. Advancements in clean energy technologies, such as solar, wind, and hydropower, have made them more affordable and accessible. Scaling up these technologies not only reduces carbon emissions but also generates new jobs and economic growth. Furthermore, transitioning to a low-carbon economy fosters innovation and creativity in various sectors, providing significant opportunities for resource efficiency and sustainable development.

4. Policy and regulatory considerations:

Government policies play a crucial role in incentivizing the transition to a low-carbon economy. By implementing carbon pricing mechanisms, renewable energy targets, and stricter environmental regulations, governments can create a conducive environment for sustainable practices. Additionally, promoting research and development in clean energy technologies and providing subsidies or tax incentives for renewable energy investments are vital means to facilitate the transition. A collaborative approach involving private sector engagement and international cooperation is essential for effective policy formulation and implementation.

5. Just transition and social equity:

A just transition is paramount to ensure that the burdens and benefits of transitioning to a low-carbon economy are fairly distributed. Displaced workers from fossil fuel industries must be provided with adequate support, retraining, and opportunities in the clean energy sector. Additionally, equitable access to renewable energy and energy efficiency measures should be prioritized to prevent exacerbating existing social inequalities. By addressing these social equity concerns, governments and policymakers can garner greater public support and bring about a more sustainable and inclusive transition.

6. International cooperation and partnerships:

Transitioning to a low-carbon economy warrants close collaboration, both domestically and internationally. Sharing best practices, technical expertise, and financial resources can significantly accelerate the transition process. International agreements, such as the Paris Agreement, provide a framework for global cooperation on climate action and low-carbon development. Building partnerships between governments, businesses, research institutions, and civil society organizations is vital for harnessing collective wisdom and resources to tackle the multifaceted challenges of transition.

THE TRANSITION FROM fossil fuels to a low-carbon economy is an imperative for a sustainable and resilient future. The urgency of addressing climate change, the health impacts of air pollution, and the need for sustainable development demand concerted efforts from all stakeholders. While challenges exist, the abundant opportunities, technological advancements, policy frameworks, and cooperation mechanisms point toward a viable path forward. By comprehensively addressing the challenges, advocating for social equity, and fostering international cooperation, the transition to a low-carbon economy can be accomplished, paving the way for a brighter and cleaner future.

- Analysis of the challenges and opportunities of reducing dependence on fossil fuels

Analysis of the Challenges and Opportunities of Reducing Dependence on Fossil Fuels

THE GLOBAL DEPENDENCY on fossil fuels has led to numerous environmental, social, and economic challenges. As society wakes up to the need for sustainable energy alternatives, the opportunities and challenges of reducing dependence on fossil fuels come to the forefront. This analysis delves deep into these aspects, shedding light on the complex dynamics involved in this transition.

1. Environmental Challenges:

The burning of fossil fuels is a major contributor to greenhouse gas emissions and climate change. As such, the overdependence on these resources poses serious environmental challenges. Transitioning to renewable energy sources, such as solar, wind, hydro, or geothermal power, is a key opportunity to mitigate these concerns and reduce carbon emissions. However, the infrastructure required for implementing these sources on a large scale often faces resistance, requiring careful planning and social acceptance.

2. Economic Challenges:

Fossil fuels have historically played a pivotal role in the global economy. Reducing dependence on fossil fuels implies a paradigm shift that presents economic challenges. The fossil fuel industry contributes significantly to job creation and economic growth in many countries. Transitioning away from this framework requires a coordinated effort to ensure a just and inclusive transition. Job losses and economic impact in regions built around fossil fuel industries must be addressed through investments in renewable energy sectors and re-skilling programs, offering opportunities for a smooth transition without disrupting economies.

3. Technological Challenges:

Transitioning to renewable energy sources demands significant advancements and breakthroughs in technology. Challenges include efficiently storing and distributing renewable energy, improving grid infrastructure to support intermittent sources, and increasing the overall energy efficiency. Efforts should be directed towards research and development, incentivizing innovation, and fostering collaborations between academia, industry, and governments. These endeavors create opportunities for technological advancement, job creation, and promoting sustainability.

4. Policy and Regulatory Challenges:

Government policies and regulations play a crucial role in shaping energy transitions. Incentives for renewable energy adoption, removing subsidies for fossil fuels, and implementing stringent emission regulations are crucial steps towards reducing dependence on fossil fuels. However, political challenges often hinder the implementation of ambitious policies due to lobbying from fossil fuel industries and resistance from vested interests. Strengthening political will and garnering public support is key to navigating policy and regulatory challenges.

5. Social Challenges:

Societal attitudes and behaviors are essential in driving the transition towards sustainable energy systems. A significant challenge lies in overcoming apathy, lack of awareness, and public skepticism towards renewable energy alternatives. Public education campaigns and awareness programs can help address these challenges, creating opportunities for behavioral changes and fostering acceptance of renewable energy technologies. Engaging communities in decision-making processes and ensuring inclusivity are crucial steps towards building trust and social acceptance.

⎯⎯⎯⎯⎯◉⎯⎯⎯⎯⎯

REDUCING DEPENDENCE on fossil fuels presents a plethora of challenges spanning environmental, economic, technological, policy, and social spheres. However, within these challenges also lie tremendous opportunities for sustainable development, innovation, and economic growth. Addressing these challenges requires global collaboration, robust policies, technological advancements, social engagement, and public participation. By embracing these opportunities and overcoming associated hurdles, societies can pave the way towards a greener and more sustainable future.

- Discussion of possible alternatives such as biofuels and hydrogen energy

Biofuels and hydrogen energy have gained significant attention as potential alternatives to fossil fuels, and their widespread adoption seems increasingly plausible. In this discussion, we will explore these alternatives, considering their potential benefits, drawbacks, and the challenges associated with their implementation.

To begin with, biofuels are renewable energy sources derived from organic matter such as plants, algae, or animal waste. They are typically categorized into two main types: ethanol and biodiesel. Ethanol, commonly produced from crops like corn and sugarcane, can be blended with gasoline and used to fuel conventional vehicles. Biodiesel, on the other hand, is made by the reaction of vegetable oils or animal fats with methanol or ethanol and can be used as a substitute for diesel fuel.

The use of biofuels presents several advantages. Firstly, they are low in carbon emissions, helping to alleviate climate change concerns. Unlike fossil fuels, burning biofuels only releases the carbon dioxide (CO_2) absorbed during the organic material's growth cycle, making them a carbon-neutral option. Additionally, biofuels promote energy security by reducing dependence on finite oil reserves from politically vulnerable regions.

However, the use of biofuels also faces significant challenges. One major concern involves the competition for land and resources with food production. When large areas of arable land are diverted for biofuel crop cultivation, it can impact food availability and raise food prices. Another challenge includes the excessive use of water, fertilizers, and pesticides during the cultivation process, potentially leading to increased environmental degradation. Moreover, the overall efficiency of biofuels is still being debated since the energy inputs required for cultivation, processing, and transportation can be substantial.

Hydrogen energy offers another promising alternative to fossil fuels. Hydrogen can be produced through various methods, including steam methane reforming, electrolysis, and biomass gasification. Once produced, it can either be used directly as a fuel or converted into electricity through fuel cells.

Hydrogen has several advantages worth considering. Firstly, it is the most abundant element in the universe and can be readily obtained from water or natural gas. Moreover, when hydrogen is burned or used in fuel cells, the only byproduct generated is water, making it a clean and emission-free energy source. Furthermore, hydrogen offers long-term energy storage potential, which is essential for intermittent energy sources like solar and wind power.

However, there are significant challenges associated with hydrogen energy implementation. Firstly, hydrogen production is energy-intensive, often relying on fossil fuels, which indirectly leads to carbon emissions. To address this issue, dedicated renewable energy sources should be utilized for hydrogen production. Additionally, hydrogen storage and transportation present considerable difficulties due to its low density. Development of safe and efficient storage technologies, such as high-pressure gas cylinders or chemical carriers, is necessary for its widespread adoption. Lastly, building the necessary infrastructure, including hydrogen refueling stations and distribution networks, poses a considerable financial and logistical challenge.

In conclusion, biofuels and hydrogen energy represent promising alternatives to fossil fuels with several benefits, including reduced greenhouse gas emissions and enhanced energy independence. However, the widespread adoption of these alternatives requires addressing challenges such as land competition, resource requirements, efficiency concerns, hydrogen production emissions, storage considerations, and infrastructure development. Policymakers, scientists, and industry stakeholders need to work collaboratively to drive technological advancements and ensure the sustainable implementation of these alternatives in our quest for a cleaner and more sustainable energy future.

- Exploration of strategies for a smooth transition to a low-carbon economy

Exploration of Strategies for a Smooth Transition to a Low-Carbon Economy

IN LIGHT OF THE GROWING concern over climate change, a global shift towards a low-carbon economy has become not only a necessity but also an economic and social opportunity. This transition involves reducing carbon emissions, developing renewable energy sources, and pursuing sustainable business practices. However, achieving a smooth transition requires careful planning, effective policymaking, and cooperation between governments, businesses, and civil society. This article explores various strategies to facilitate a seamless and successful transition to a low-carbon economy.

1. Setting Ambitious Emission Reduction Targets:

One essential strategy for a smooth transition to a low-carbon economy is setting clear, ambitious emission reduction targets. Governments must commit to binding agreements, such as the Paris Agreement, and strive to exceed initial commitments. These targets provide a long-term vision, heighten accountability, and enable effective planning and allocation of resources to meet climate goals.

2. Phasing out Fossil Fuel Subsidies:

Phasing out fossil fuel subsidies is crucial for encouraging the adoption of low-carbon alternatives. By redirecting subsidies to support renewable energy sources, governments can incentivize the transition to cleaner technologies. This strategy not only contributes to emission reduction but also enhances the economic viability of sustainable alternatives in the market.

3. Encouraging Research and Innovation:

Investing in research and innovation plays a vital role in a smooth transition to a low-carbon economy. Governments should collaborate with academia and industry to drive technological advancements, helping to accelerate the development and commercialization of renewable energy technologies. By providing financial support and intellectual property protection, policymakers can foster a culture of innovation that drives sustainability initiatives across sectors.

4. Implementing Carbon Pricing Initiatives:

Carbon pricing mechanisms, such as carbon taxes and cap-and-trade systems, can incentivize businesses to reduce their carbon footprint. By placing a financial cost on emitting greenhouse gases, these initiatives encourage industries to invest in cleaner technologies, energy efficiency, and responsible practices. Properly designed and carefully phased-in carbon pricing initiatives can help shift market dynamics, encouraging businesses to transition to low-carbon alternatives gradually.

5. Prioritizing Renewable Energy Development:

The accelerated development and deployment of renewable energy sources is a critical strategy for achieving a low-carbon economy. Governments must implement supportive policies, such as feed-in tariffs and grants for research and development, to accelerate the investment in and installation of renewable energy infrastructure. Collaboration between governments, businesses, and electricity grid operators is necessary to ensure the integration of renewable energy sources with existing grids and enhance the energy sector's resilience.

6. Promoting Green Financing and Investment:

Enabling access to affordable financing for green projects is essential for the smooth transition to a low-carbon economy. Governments can play a crucial role in creating financial mechanisms and institutions that provide incentives and support for sustainable investments. Encouraging public-private partnerships and leveraging the potential of green bonds, carbon markets, and impact investments are effective strategies to attract and mobilize private capital towards low-carbon initiatives.

7. Fostering Public Awareness and Engagement:

Engaging and educating the public on the benefits of a low-carbon economy is a fundamental strategy for achieving widespread support and participation. Governments must launch comprehensive communication campaigns to raise awareness of climate change impacts and the positive impacts of transitioning to a low-carbon economy. Moreover, actively involving civil society organizations, NGOs, and local communities in decision-making processes fosters ownership and encourages bottom-up initiatives that contribute to a smooth transition.

<hr>

TO SUCCESSFULLY TRANSITION to a low-carbon economy, it is crucial to adopt and implement a combination of these strategies. While investment in renewable energy and technological advancements remains central, effective policymaking and active collaboration between stakeholders are equally important. By taking ambitious actions, fostering innovation, and actively engaging the public, governments and businesses can pave the way for a sustainable future, ensuring a smooth and successful low-carbon economy transition.

Chapter 7: Sustainable Agriculture and Land Use

In today's rapidly changing world, sustainability has become a pressing concern, especially when it comes to agriculture and land use. The way we grow our food and utilize our land can have profound impacts on our environment, economy, and society. This chapter delves into the concept of sustainable agriculture, exploring its principles, benefits, and challenges. Additionally, it examines sustainable land use practices that can help protect natural resources and ensure long-term food security.

1. The Concept of Sustainable Agriculture:

Sustainable agriculture refers to the practice of producing food in a way that sustains natural resources, minimizes environmental impact, and supports rural livelihoods. It aims to meet the needs of present generations without compromising the ability of future generations to meet their own needs. Key principles of sustainable agriculture include:

1.1. Conservation of natural resources:

Sustainable agriculture focuses on preserving soil fertility, water quality, and biodiversity. It promotes practices such as soil conservation, precision farming, organic fertilization, and agroforestry. By minimizing the use of synthetic inputs and maximizing ecological interactions, sustainable agriculture reduces pollution and protects natural ecosystems.

1.2. Economic viability:

Farmers practicing sustainable agriculture aim to achieve economic profitability, ensuring a fair income that allows for investment and improvement in farming techniques. By diversifying production and adopting innovative marketing strategies, farmers can enhance their profitability and resilience to market fluctuations.

1.3. Social equity:

Sustainable agriculture recognizes the importance of social justice within the agricultural sector, supporting fair trade and equal opportunities for all. It promotes rural development, gender equality, and the improvement of living and working conditions for farmers and laborers.

2. Benefits of Sustainable Agriculture:

The adoption of sustainable agricultural practices offers numerous benefits at various levels:

2.1. Environmental benefits:

By minimizing the use of chemical inputs, sustainable agriculture minimizes soil erosion, land degradation, and water pollution. It also helps sequester carbon in soils, mitigating climate change impacts. Furthermore, sustainable farming practices protect biodiversity, promote habitat conservation, and contribute to wildlife preservation.

2.2. Economic benefits:

Sustainable agriculture can lead to increased farm profits through reduced production costs and enhanced market access. By diversifying crops, farmers can adapt to changing market demands and reduce the vulnerability associated with monocultures. Sustainable agriculture can also improve rural livelihoods by creating job opportunities and providing income stability.

2.3. Social benefits:

Sustainable agriculture fosters community development, improving food security, education, and healthcare for rural populations. It empowers farmers, enabling them to have more control over their land and resources. Moreover, sustainable farming practices can enhance consumer health by providing nutritious and safe food.

3. Challenges in Promoting Sustainable Agriculture:

While the concept of sustainable agriculture is compelling, there are several challenges that hinder its widespread adoption:

3.1. Transition costs:

Transitioning from conventional to sustainable agriculture often requires significant upfront investment. Farmers may need to invest in new equipment, training, and infrastructure. Lack of financial resources and credit access can limit the expansion of sustainable agricultural practices.

3.2. Knowledge and information gaps:

Sustainable agriculture involves applying scientific knowledge and embracing innovative approaches. However, many farmers lack access to the necessary training, technical expertise, and research findings. Bridging these knowledge gaps is critical to encourage the adoption of sustainable techniques.

3.3. Policy and market incentives:

Governments need to create supportive policies and provide financial incentives to encourage sustainable practices. Lack of such policies may deter farmers from adopting sustainable agriculture despite its benefits. Additionally, an absence of sustainable product certifications and consumer demand can limit market opportunities for sustainable agricultural products.

━━━◉━━━

ADOPTING SUSTAINABLE agriculture and land use practices is crucial for ensuring long-term food security, protecting natural resources, and promoting the well-being of farmers and rural communities. By embracing sustainability principles, minimizing environmental impact, and considering economic viability and social equity, we can move towards a more resilient and sustainable agricultural system. Overcoming challenges through policy support and knowledge transfer is essential to achieve widespread adoption of sustainable practices and build a brighter and more sustainable future for generations to come.

- Illumination of the impact of the agricultural sector on global warming

The agricultural sector plays a crucial role in global warming due to its significant contributions to greenhouse gas emissions and deforestation. These factors, coupled with the growing demands of the world's population and changing dietary patterns, have made it necessary to assess the impact of agriculture on climate change.

One of the primary ways in which agriculture contributes to global warming is through the emission of greenhouse gases. Livestock farming, large-scale arable farming, and the use of synthetic fertilizers all release substantial amounts of greenhouse gases into the atmosphere. For example, the production of methane, a potent greenhouse gas, is attributed to the digestive processes of ruminant animals like cattle and sheep. Additionally, the excessive use of synthetic fertilizers leads to the emission of nitrous oxide, another potent greenhouse gas.

Deforestation is another significant consequence of the agricultural sector. Forests play a crucial role in stabilizing global climate patterns by absorbing carbon dioxide and releasing oxygen. However, large tracts of land are continuously cleared for agricultural expansion, especially for livestock farming and cultivating crops like soybeans and palm oil. This deforestation not only releases stored carbon dioxide into the atmosphere but also disrupts the natural carbon sink, exacerbating the effects of global warming.

Moreover, the agricultural sector is responsible for large-scale water consumption, contributing to freshwater scarcity and indirectly exacerbating global warming. The excessive use of irrigation for crop cultivation leads to the depletion of freshwater resources, which in turn increases competition for water and heightens the risk of conflicts over water rights. Climate change further compounds this issue by altering rainfall patterns and exacerbating drought conditions in many parts of the world.

Additionally, the transportation and distribution of agricultural produce significantly contribute to greenhouse gas emissions. The global food supply chain, with its reliance on long-distance transportation, refrigeration, and the use of fossil fuels for machinery and processing, effectively increases the carbon footprint of the agricultural sector. As the demand for food continues to grow, especially with the rise in urbanization and changing dietary patterns, these emissions are further amplified.

Finally, the depletion of soil health and biodiversity resulting from intensive agricultural practices has indirect implications for global warming. Soil erosion, loss of natural habitat, and decreased diversity in crop species can disrupt important ecological cycles, further pushing the world towards an unsustainable future. It is crucial to recognize and address these interconnected issues in order to mitigate the impact of agriculture on global warming.

In conclusion, the agricultural sector significantly impacts global warming through its greenhouse gas emissions, deforestation, intense water consumption, transportation logistics, and soil degradation. As the global population grows, it is imperative to transition to sustainable agricultural practices, such as regenerative agriculture and precision farming, to minimize these negative effects on the environment. By implementing more environmentally friendly approaches and finding alternatives to current unsustainable practices, we can achieve a more sustainable food system and mitigate climate change.

- Discussion of sustainable farming practices to minimize greenhouse gas contributions

Sustainable farming practices have become an important topic of discussion in recent years, partly due to the urgent need to minimize greenhouse gas (GHG) contributions. Agriculture is a significant source of GHG emissions, with its various practices accounting for approximately 11% of global emissions. However, by implementing sustainable farming techniques, farmers can reduce their environmental impact and contribute to mitigating climate change.

One crucial aspect of sustainable farming is minimizing the use of synthetic fertilizers. These fertilizers release nitrous oxide (N_2O), a potent GHG, into the atmosphere. Farmers can employ methods such as crop rotation and cover cropping to provide natural sources of nitrogen and enhance soil fertility. By alternating leguminous plants with cereal crops, for example, farmers can capitalize on the nitrogen-fixing abilities of legumes, reducing the need for synthetic fertilizers.

The management of livestock also plays a significant role in minimizing GHG emissions. Ruminant animals, such as cattle and sheep, are responsible for methane (CH_4) emissions through enteric fermentation. Incorporating practices like rotational grazing and proper dietary management can significantly reduce these emissions. Rotational grazing allows pasturelands to recover, resulting in improved forage quality and lower methane emissions.

In addition to addressing nitrogen and methane emissions, sustainable farming practices also focus on sequestering carbon dioxide (CO_2) from the atmosphere. Practices like agroforestry and conservation tillage help in retaining and building soil organic matter, which acts as a carbon sink. Planting trees alongside crops not only facilitates biodiversity but also enables carbon capture by increasing the overall carbon storage capacity of the landscape.

Moreover, sustainable water management techniques can also contribute to mitigating climate change impacts. Implementing precision irrigation systems, such as drip irrigation, reduces water waste and energy consumption. This, in turn, reduces the GHG emissions associated with water pumping and distribution.

Alongside these farming practices, renewable energy sources should be encouraged in agriculture to lessen reliance on fossil fuels. The installation of solar panels or wind turbines on farms can provide clean energy, powering farm operations and reducing overall emissions. Additionally, anaerobic digesters can be employed to convert organic waste into biogas, an alternative to traditional energy sources.

Furthermore, sustainable farming practices involve a holistic approach that extends beyond solely reducing GHG emissions. It encompasses the preservation of soil health, promotion of biodiversity, and protection of water resources. Developing regenerative farming systems that focus on improving the overall ecosystem resilience and ecological balance is fundamental.

Transitioning to sustainable farming practices may entail challenges for farmers, as they need to alter their traditional approaches and adopt new techniques. However, governments and organizations can play a crucial role in encouraging and supporting this transition by providing financial incentives, technical assistance, and educational resources.

In conclusion, sustainable farming practices offer significant opportunities to minimize the greenhouse gas contributions from agricultural activities. By avoiding the excessive use of synthetic fertilizers, managing livestock, promoting carbon sequestration, employing efficient water management strategies, and transitioning to renewable energy sources, farmers can reduce their carbon footprint while improving overall sustainability. Embracing sustainable farming practices is not only crucial for mitigating climate change but also for ensuring long-term food security and environmental well-being.

- Examination of strategies for better land-use planning and avoiding deforestation

Land-use planning and the prevention of deforestation are critical issues in today's world. With the increasing global population and the growing demand for resources, it has become imperative to develop effective strategies to ensure sustainable land-use practices and mitigate deforestation.

One of the most significant challenges in land-use planning is striking a balance between meeting human needs and preserving natural ecosystems. Often, economic development takes precedence over environmental conservation, leading to deforestation and habitat destruction. However, there are several strategies that can be employed to better manage land use and minimize deforestation.

Firstly, comprehensive spatial planning is crucial for effective land-use management. This involves identifying and zoning different land-use types based on ecological, economic, and social considerations. By designating protected areas, such as national parks and nature reserves, the most ecologically valuable landscapes can be conserved, minimizing the impact of deforestation. Additionally, regional planning can promote sustainable agriculture and forestry practices, ensuring that land resources are used efficiently and sustainably.

Furthermore, engaging local communities in land-use planning is essential for success. Communities that depend on forests for livelihoods often contribute to deforestation through illegal logging, subsistence agriculture, and unsustainable resource extraction. By involving these communities in decision-making processes and providing economic incentives for sustainable practices, their participation in deforestation can be reduced. This can be achieved through initiatives like community forestry, where local communities are granted rights and responsibilities in managing forest resources.

Policy interventions also play a significant role in land-use planning and deforestation prevention. Governments should implement legislation that aims to protect forests and control land conversion for commercial purposes. These policies should include strict enforcement, penalties for illegal activities, and incentives for sustainable practices. Additionally, international agreements like the United Nations REDD+ program (Reducing Emissions from Deforestation and Forest Degradation) provide financial incentives to countries that reduce deforestation rates and enhance forest conservation efforts.

Innovative technology can also support improved land-use planning and forest management. Geographic Information Systems (GIS) and remote sensing techniques can provide valuable data on land cover, forest extent, and potential areas of deforestation. This information can aid decision-makers in identifying areas at risk and implementing preventive measures. Moreover, satellite monitoring can enable real-time monitoring of deforestation activities, facilitating early intervention and ensuring timely enforcement.

Education and awareness-raising campaigns are powerful tools in promoting sustainable land use and preventing deforestation. By emphasizing the importance of forests for climate regulation, biodiversity conservation, and human well-being, people can be motivated to take action. Through environmental education, stakeholders can learn about sustainable land-use practices, the benefits of forest conservation, and the consequences of deforestation. This can lead to a more informed and responsible approach to land-use planning, driving toward a greener and more sustainable future.

In summary, the examination of strategies for better land-use planning and deforestation prevention is of paramount importance. By implementing comprehensive spatial planning, involving local communities, enacting effective policies, leveraging technology, and raising awareness, it is possible to strike a balance between human needs and the preservation of natural ecosystems. Only through proactive and sustainable land-use planning can we avoid further deforestation and safeguard our planet's invaluable resources for future generations.

Chapter 8: Carbon Capture and Storage Technologies

Carbon capture and storage (CCS) technologies play a crucial role in mitigating climate change by reducing greenhouse gas emissions from various industries. These technologies capture carbon dioxide (CO_2) from point sources such as power plants and industrial facilities, preventing it from being released into the atmosphere. The captured CO_2 is then transported to storage sites and stored securely underground for long periods. In this chapter, we explore CCS technologies in detail, including the different methods, challenges, and potential benefits.

1. Types of Carbon Capture Technologies:

There are three primary types of CCS technologies: post-combustion, pre-combustion, and oxy-fuel combustion. In post-combustion capture, CO_2 is captured from flue gases after fuel combustion. Pre-combustion capture involves converting hydrocarbon fuels into hydrogen and CO_2 before combustion, with only CO_2 being captured. Oxy-fuel combustion replaces air with pure oxygen during the combustion process, producing a flue gas primarily composed of CO_2, which can be readily captured.

2. Carbon Capture Techniques:

Various techniques are employed to capture CO_2 in CCS technologies. These include absorption, adsorption, and membrane separation. Absorption involves dissolving CO_2 in a liquid solvent, whereas adsorption involves attaching CO_2 molecules to solid surfaces. Membrane separation utilizes selectively permeable membranes to separate CO_2 from other gases. Each technique has its advantages and disadvantages, and the choice depends on factors such as cost, efficiency, and scalability.

3. Transporting and Storing Captured CO_2:

Once the CO_2 is captured, it needs to be transported to storage sites. Pipelines are the most commonly used method for transportation, often repurposing existing natural gas pipelines. The CO_2 is compressed and injected into deep geological formations for storage. These formations include depleted oil and gas fields, saline aquifers, and deep coal seams. Secure storage is essential to prevent CO2 leakage back into the atmosphere and to ensure the long-term effectiveness of CCS.

4. Challenges of Carbon Capture and Storage:

While CCS technologies present promising solutions, several challenges hinder their widespread deployment. The high costs associated with capturing, transporting, and storing CO2 remain a significant barrier. Additionally, the scale required for large-scale deployment adds further complexities. Regulatory and policy frameworks also need to be developed to address liability and long-term monitoring requirements. Public acceptance and engagement in CCS projects, as well as potential environmental risks associated with storage, must be thoroughly considered.

5. Potential Benefits of Carbon Capture and Storage:

Despite the challenges, carbon capture and storage offer significant benefits in the fight against climate change. CCS technologies can potentially reduce CO2 emissions by up to 90%, making them a crucial tool in decarbonizing industries heavily dependent on fossil fuels. Furthermore, CCS allows countries to utilize their abundant fossil fuel resources while achieving emissions reduction goals. The stored CO2 can also enhance oil recovery in some cases, providing additional economic benefits.

⎯⎯⎯◉⎯⎯⎯

CARBON CAPTURE AND storage technologies have the potential to play a pivotal role in addressing climate change and reducing greenhouse gas emissions. By capturing and storing CO2 from various industries, these technologies offer a pathway to a more sustainable and low-carbon future. However, substantial advancements are required in terms of cost efficiency, scalability, and public perception to ensure the widespread deployment of CCS technologies. With continued research and development, CCS can become a vital component of a comprehensive climate change mitigation strategy.

- Introduction to the concept of carbon capture and storage as a mitigation strategy

Carbon capture and storage (CCS) is an innovative and promising technology that involves the capture, transportation, and storage of carbon dioxide (CO_2) emissions from various sources, such as power plants and industrial facilities. It has gained significant attention in recent years as a potential mitigation strategy for combating climate change.

The concept of CCS revolves around the concept of reducing greenhouse gas emissions, particularly CO_2, by capturing it before it is released into the atmosphere. This captured CO_2 is then transported and securely stored underground, typically in geological formations like depleted oil and gas fields or deep saline aquifers.

One of the primary aspects of CCS is the capture of carbon dioxide. There are different technological options for capturing CO_2, including post-combustion capture, pre-combustion capture, and oxy-combustion. Post-combustion capture involves isolating CO_2 from the exhaust gases of power plants, while pre-combustion capture involves the removal of CO_2 from hydrocarbon fuels before they are utilized for energy production. Oxy-combustion, on the other hand, involves the combustion of fuel in pure oxygen and resulting flue gas, mainly composed of CO_2, is then captured.

Once the CO_2 is captured, it needs to be transported to storage sites. This transportation process, often accomplished through pipelines, requires careful planning and monitoring to ensure the safe transportation of the captured CO_2. The distances of transportation can vary greatly depending on the location of the capture source and the availability of suitable storage sites.

The last step in CCS is the storage of CO_2 deep underground. This is typically done in specific geological formations that have the capacity to retain the CO_2 securely. Depleted oil and gas fields provide an ideal storage option as they have already demonstrated their ability to trap and store hydrocarbons for millions of years. Deep saline aquifers, which are layers of porous rock filled with salty water deep underground, can also serve as potential storage reservoirs.

One of the key advantages of CCS is its potential to significantly reduce CO2 emissions from various industrial processes. By capturing and storing the CO2 emissions that would have otherwise been released into the atmosphere, CCS can play a crucial role in preventing climate change caused by greenhouse gas emissions. It can also be deployed alongside renewable energy sources to provide a more immediate and effective transition to clean energy while reducing the reliance on fossil fuels.

However, the implementation of CCS faces several challenges. The technology is still considered relatively expensive and requires significant investment for its widespread deployment. Moreover, the capturing and storage processes require careful measurement, monitoring, and verification to ensure the safety and permanence of the stored CO2. Additionally, the potential environmental impacts and public acceptance of CCS, particularly in terms of storage site selection and the potential for CO2 leakage, must be carefully addressed.

In conclusion, carbon capture and storage offers a promising strategy for mitigating CO2 emissions and combating climate change. It provides an opportunity to effectively reduce greenhouse gas emissions from various sources, including power plants and industrial facilities. While challenges exist in terms of cost, safety, and public acceptance, continued research and development in CCS can further improve its viability and contribute to a more sustainable future.

- Explanation of different technologies used for capturing and storing carbon dioxide

The world is currently facing one of the most pressing global challenges – climate change. As greenhouse gas emissions continue to rise, researchers and scientists are exploring various technologies to mitigate the impact of carbon dioxide (CO_2) on the environment. Among these technologies are groundbreaking methods for capturing and storing carbon dioxide. In this article, we will delve into the different technologies used for capturing and storing CO_2, examining their mechanisms, advantages, and limitations.

Carbon capture and storage (CCS) systems are designed to reduce CO_2 emissions from industrial processes and power generation, particularly from large-scale stationary sources. CCS involves three main steps: capturing CO_2, transporting it to a storage site, and storing it securely underground. Let's explore the technologies associated with each of these steps.

First, let's discuss the capture stage. There are three primary methods employed to capture CO_2: post-combustion capture, pre-combustion capture, and oxy-fuel combustion.

Post-combustion capture is the most commonly used method. It involves capturing CO_2 after fossil fuels have been burned to generate energy. Technology such as absorption systems, using solvents like amine, is utilized to separate CO_2 from the flue gas emitted during energy production. Once separated, the CO_2 can be compressed and transported.

Pre-combustion capture, on the other hand, occurs before the combustion process takes place. In this method, fossil fuels are first heated with steam, resulting in a fuel gas mixture comprising hydrogen and carbon monoxide. The CO_2 can be removed from this mixture, leaving behind hydrogen to generate energy with significantly reduced emissions.

Oxy-fuel combustion is a less common technique where fossil fuels are burned in pure oxygen or oxygen-enriched environments to produce flue gas consisting mainly of CO_2 and water vapor. The water vapor is then condensed, making it easier to separate the CO2 from the gas stream. This method is considered more efficient as it produces a higher concentration of CO2.

Once captured, the next step is to transport the CO2 for storage. Two main methods are currently employed: pipeline transport and ship transport.

Pipeline systems are widely used for transporting CO2 due to their cost-effectiveness and efficiency. Similar to how natural gas is distributed through pipelines, CO2 can be transported in a gaseous or supercritical state through specially designed pipelines. These pipelines ensure secure and reliable delivery of the captured CO2 to storage sites. Alternatively, ship transport is utilized when pipelines are not feasible, such as in distant or isolated regions. However, it requires more energy and infrastructure to convert gaseous CO2 into a liquid state for transportation.

Finally, let's move on to the storage stage. Secure geological storage is currently the most viable option for long-term CO2 storage. The two primary storage methods are saline aquifer storage and depleted oil and gas reservoir storage.

In saline aquifer storage, CO2 is injected into deep underground rock formations, typically porous sandstone or limestone. These formations, located thousands of meters below the surface, have the capacity to retain the CO2 securely over a long period. The injected CO2 is trapped beneath impermeable rock layers, preventing its release into the atmosphere.

Depleted oil and gas reservoirs offer another storage solution. These reservoirs have been exhausted of their fossil fuel resources, leaving behind naturally occurring formations that can be utilized to store CO2. Similar to saline aquifers, the CO2 is injected into these reservoirs and safely trapped beneath impervious cap rocks, ensuring no leakage.

While CCS technologies hold great potential in the fight against climate change, they still face several challenges. The implementation and scaling up of these technologies require significant investment and policy support. Additionally, issues like leakage of stored CO2, the high cost of capture and transport, and public acceptance need to be addressed for effective deployment on a larger scale.

In conclusion, the technologies used for capturing and storing carbon dioxide are crucial in mitigating the impact of greenhouse gas emissions. Through various capture methods, efficient transport methods, and secure geological storage, we have the potential to reduce CO2 emissions and combat climate change. However, further research and development, alongside supportive policies and investments, are essential to achieve widespread deployment of these technologies and move towards a greener future.

- Evaluation of the feasibility and scalability of these technologies in combating global warming

Evaluation of the Feasibility and Scalability of These Technologies in Combating Global Warming

WITH THE INCREASING concerns about climate change and its potential impacts on the planet, there is a growing need for technologies that can effectively combat global warming. In this evaluation, we will analyze the feasibility and scalability of various technologies that have the potential to address this pressing issue. By assessing their current state of development, their environmental impact, and their potential for widespread implementation, we aim to determine which of these technologies hold the greatest promise in fighting global warming.

1. Renewable Energy Sources:

Usage of renewable energy sources, such as wind, solar, and hydro, has seen significant growth in recent years. These technologies have considerable potential in combating global warming by drastically reducing carbon emissions associated with traditional fossil fuel-based energy generation. The feasibility of renewable energy sources is evident through their off-grid implementation, and the continued advancement of their efficiency and cost reduction. Continued investment and policy support will be necessary for the large-scale deployment of these technologies.

2. Energy Storage Systems:

Renewable energy sources are intermittent in nature, meaning their generation varies based on prevailing conditions. Developing robust energy storage systems is crucial to utilize these renewable energy sources effectively. Battery technologies, such as lithium-ion and flow batteries, are rapidly advancing and becoming more economically feasible. The scalability of energy storage systems is primarily dependent on improving their storage capacities and decreasing costs. Research and development in this field must continue to ensure widespread deployment and scalability.

3. Carbon Capture, Utilization, and Storage (CCUS):

CCUS technologies offer the potential to reduce carbon dioxide (CO2) emissions from large-scale industrial processes and power plants. There are several methods being investigated, including direct air capture, bioenergy with carbon capture and storage, and ocean fertilization. While the feasibility of CCUS technologies has been demonstrated in small-scale experiments, the scalability and associated costs remain major challenges. Governments and industries must offer incentives and invest in research to bring down costs and make these technologies economically viable.

4. Green Building Design:

Construction and operation of buildings contribute significantly to global CO2 emissions. Green building design aims to minimize energy usage, use renewable materials, and reduce emissions associated with the building lifecycle. Several technologies, such as smart lighting systems, efficient heating and cooling, energy-efficient windows, and insulation, are already available to improve the sustainability of buildings. Further research and development are required to enhance the feasibility and cost-effectiveness of green building practices, as well as to develop scalable solutions for retrofitting existing buildings.

5. Advanced Transportation Technologies:

Transportation is another major contributor to global emissions, primarily through the use of fossil fuel-powered vehicles. Developing advanced transportation technologies, including electric vehicles (EVs), hydrogen fuel cells, and sustainable biofuels, offer potential solutions to reduce carbon emissions. The feasibility of these technologies is demonstrated through the increasing adoption of EVs and the development of charging infrastructure. Scaling up EV adoption and overcoming limitations and costs associated with hydrogen fuel cells and sustainable biofuels are key future challenges.

IN EVALUATING THE FEASIBILITY and scalability of technologies to combat global warming, it is clear that considering multi-dimensional solutions is essential. Our analysis reveals that renewable energy sources, energy storage systems, carbon capture technologies, green building design, and advanced transportation technologies all hold promise in tackling global warming. While some technologies are further along in terms of scalability and feasibility, ongoing investment, research, and government support are necessary to accelerate their development and deployment. Furthermore, the combination of these technologies and their integration into existing infrastructure will be crucial to achieving significant reductions in carbon emissions and combating global warming effectively.

Chapter 9: Climate Adaptation and Resilience

In this chapter, we delve into the critical topic of climate adaptation and resilience. As the impacts of climate change continue to unfold, it becomes increasingly important to understand how societies can adapt to and cope with these changes. This chapter provides valuable insights and information on the strategies, policies, and actions needed to build climate resilient communities.

1. Understanding Climate Adaptation:

The first section of this chapter explores the concept of climate adaptation. It delves into the fundamental principles behind adaptation and highlights the need for proactive measures to address climate risks. The chapter emphasizes that adaptation is not just about reacting to climate change impacts; it involves long-term planning, building resilient infrastructure, and developing adaptive strategies to ensure a sustainable future.

2. Climate Resilience: Building Stronger Communities:

The following section takes a closer look at climate resilience and the importance of building stronger communities. It examines the resilience of various sectors such as agriculture, water resources, and urban areas. The chapter highlights the need for integrating climate considerations into planning and emphasizes community engagement and participation in resilience-building efforts.

3. Climate Adaptation and Policies:

This section delves into the role of policies in climate adaptation. It discusses the importance of developing comprehensive and inclusive policies that address the needs of vulnerable communities. The chapter also examines various policy frameworks and strategies adopted by different countries to promote adaptation and resilience. It emphasizes the importance of coordination between government agencies, stakeholders, and the public to effectively implement and monitor adaptation policies.

4. Technological Innovations for Climate Adaptation:

In this section, the chapter explores the role of technological innovations in climate adaptation. It highlights how advancements in technologies such as remote sensing, geographic information systems (GIS), and modeling tools can enhance our understanding of climate change impacts and support decision-making processes. The chapter also discusses the importance of continued research and development in technological solutions to address climate risks effectively.

5. Financing Climate Adaptation:

The final section of the chapter sheds light on the crucial aspect of financing climate adaptation. It discusses various sources of funding, including public and private sector investments, international grants, and innovative financing mechanisms. The chapter emphasizes the need for equitable and efficient distribution of funds and the importance of financial institutions supporting climate-resilient projects.

———————◆———————

CHAPTER 9 PROVIDES a comprehensive understanding of climate adaptation and resilience. It highlights the importance of proactive measures, policies, community engagement, technological innovations, and financial support in building resilient communities. The chapter encourages readers to take action and contribute to climate adaptation efforts in their respective areas. Adaptation is no longer a choice but a necessary step towards securing our future in the face of climate change.

- Delving into the importance of adapting to the existing and future impacts of global warming

Adapting to the existing and future impacts of global warming has become an increasingly critical aspect of our lives. The urgent need to address climate change effects on our environment, societies, and economies is undeniable. As greenhouse gas emissions continue to rise, the Earth's average temperature is steadily increasing, leading to extreme weather patterns, rising sea levels, and the deterioration of natural ecosystems. In order to mitigate these challenges, we must emphasize the importance of adapting to the changing climate.

One of the fundamental reasons for embracing adaptation is that global warming is already causing tangible impacts. Heatwaves are becoming more frequent and intense, putting human health and well-being at risk. By adapting, we can implement strategies such as the implementation of heat-resistant infrastructure, designing cities with more green spaces, and developing early warning systems to mitigate the adverse effects of these extreme heat events.

Similarly, rising sea levels pose a severe threat to coastal regions. Adaptation measures such as constructing seawalls, restoring natural wetlands, and planning for managed retreat can help protect vulnerable communities from coastal flooding and erosions. Additionally, communities need to incorporate sustainable land use planning to prevent building in high-risk flood-prone areas. Adapting to this risk is essential since millions of people live in coastal areas and depend on coastal ecosystems for their livelihood.

The effects of global warming are not limited to human life and infrastructure; they also encompass natural ecosystems. Many species face amplified extinction risks due to habitat loss, changing migration patterns, and imbalances in food chains. By adopting strategies like creating ecological corridors, protecting wildlife habitats, and using sustainable agricultural practices, we will enhance the resilience of ecosystems and safeguard biodiversity. Furthermore, forest management techniques that prioritize biodiversity and community involvement can mitigate the destructive impacts of wildfires, which have become more severe and frequent.

Adapting to global warming is not only crucial in responding to current challenges but also in preparing for future impacts. Climate scientists project that the intensity and frequency of extreme weather events will continue to increase. This includes events such as hurricanes, droughts, and heavy precipitation. Communities should consider infrastructure upgrades to withstand and recover from extreme events, diversify water sources, and implement sustainable farming techniques that can withstand water scarcity. By adapting proactively, we can minimize the potential damages caused by these events and ensure society's safety and stability.

Moreover, adapting to global warming also poses economic advantages. By investing in renewable energy sources, as well as promoting energy efficiency, countries can reduce their dependency on fossil fuels and drive sustainable economic growth. Renowned economist Lord Nicholas Stern and others argue that early investments in climate adaptation and mitigation save money in the long run as the costs of inaction far exceed the cost of implementing preventive measures.

Finally, adaptation can foster a sense of global responsibility and cooperation. The impacts of global warming are no longer confined to individual countries, but rather, they affect the entire planet. Collaborative efforts to develop strategies and technologies that address climate change can create wider global unity and mutual understanding. By working together, nations can share knowledge, resources, and expertise to adapt to global warming collectively.

In conclusion, adapting to the existing and future impacts of global warming is of paramount importance. The need to mitigate the adverse effects of rising temperatures, extreme weather patterns, and ecosystem disruption requires urgent action. By embracing adaptation measures, we can build a more resilient and sustainable future for both human and natural systems. Our ability to adapt to global warming will determine our capacity to ensure the well-being of future generations and the health of our planet.

- Exploration of resilience strategies at individual, community, and national levels

Resilience, the ability to bounce back and adapt in the face of adversity, is a crucial quality for individuals, communities, and nations to possess. In times of challenges and crises, the ability to withstand hardships and recover from them becomes even more valuable. This essay explores the various strategies employed by individuals, communities, and nations to strengthen their resilience levels.

At the individual level, resilience can be fostered through various strategies. One key aspect is developing a positive mindset and optimistic outlook. This involves reframing challenges as opportunities for growth and learning. By seeing setbacks as temporary and surmountable, individuals can maintain their motivation and perseverance during difficult times. Practicing mindfulness and self-care is another important aspect of building resilience. Engaging in activities that promote mental and emotional well-being, such as exercise, meditation, or hobbies, helps individuals to cope with stressors effectively.

Furthermore, individuals can enhance their resilience by cultivating a strong support network. Having trusted friends, family, or mentors to rely on in times of need provides a crucial source of emotional support and guidance. By seeking out social connections and fostering healthy relationships, individuals are better equipped to handle adversities. In addition, having access to resources and information within their community, such as healthcare services, educational opportunities, or job assistance, further strengthens individuals' resilience.

Moving to a community level, resilience strategies expand to encompass collective mechanisms aimed at enhancing resilience for groups of individuals. Firstly, building social cohesion within the community is vital. This involves fostering a sense of belonging and mutual support among community members. Encouraging participation in community activities, organizing regular gatherings, and promoting social integration help create a supportive environment wherein individuals can rely on each other during challenging times. Strengthening community infrastructure is another critical strategy. This includes ensuring the availability of essential resources such as clean water, electricity, healthcare facilities, and transportation systems that can withstand crises or natural disasters. Developing emergency response plans and conducting drills helps communities prepare for and respond effectively to potential threats.

Engaging in community-wide education and awareness campaigns is yet another important resilience-enhancing strategy. By disseminating information on healthcare, disaster preparedness, and environmental concerns, communities can empower individuals with knowledge and tools to adapt and cope with stressors proactively. Providing education and training opportunities to community members, particularly marginalized groups, not only equips individuals with valuable skills but also fosters a sense of empowerment and self-sufficiency.

Finally, at the national level, governments play a crucial role in bolstering resilience. Policies that prioritize investment in social safety nets, healthcare systems, and education, particularly in vulnerable communities, contribute to a more resilient society. Governments also have a responsibility to establish early warning systems, disaster response protocols, and effective crisis management strategies. By having robust systems in place, nations are better equipped to respond swiftly and efficiently to crises, minimizing damage and enabling quicker recovery.

Cooperation and collaboration on regional and international levels are also important resilience-building strategies at the national level. Sharing resources, expertise, and knowledge with other countries promotes global resilience and fosters stronger support networks in times of crises. Additionally, prioritizing sustainable development practices contributes to building resilience against environmental challenges such as climate change.

In conclusion, resilience strategies at individual, community, and national levels are diverse and multi-faceted. Developing a positive mindset, maintaining social connections, and practicing self-care are crucial individual-level strategies. Communities can foster resilience through enhancing social cohesion, strengthening infrastructure, and promoting education and awareness initiatives. Governments, on the other hand, play a vital role in creating an environment conducive to resilience through policy-making, infrastructure development, disaster preparedness, and international collaboration. By embracing these strategies, individuals, communities, and nations can fortify their ability to withstand adversity and build a more resilient future.

- Case studies demonstrating successful climate adaptation initiatives

Case Study 1: Floating Gardens in Bangladesh

Bangladesh, one of the most vulnerable countries to climate change, has been facing the annual threat of flooding due to rising sea levels. In response to this challenge, a non-profit organization called Shidhulai Swanirvar Sangstha introduced an innovative adaptation initiative known as floating gardens.

The concept behind floating gardens is simple yet effective. Bamboo platforms are constructed, on which a layer of hyacinth, organic debris, and rotting aquatic weeds are placed to form the base. Soil is then added, followed by cultivation of vegetables such as tomatoes, cucumbers, and beans.

The success of floating gardens lies in their ability to withstand flooding. As the sea levels rise, the gardens float, ensuring a continuous food supply for the communities living in the Sunamganj region. In addition, these gardens also serve as a means of livelihood, generating income for the local communities through the sale of excess produce.

Case Study 2: Urban Heat Islands in Tokyo, Japan

Tokyo, a densely populated city, is faced with the challenge of urban heat islands, where temperatures in urban areas are significantly higher than in surrounding rural areas due to the heat-absorbing nature of concrete and the lack of green spaces. In response, the Tokyo Metropolitan Government implemented a successful climate adaptation initiative known as the "Cool Biz" campaign.

Under this initiative, the government encourages offices and public spaces to reduce their air conditioning usage by raising the recommended indoor temperature to 28 degrees Celsius (82.4 degrees Fahrenheit). Additionally, employees are encouraged to dress smartly but in cool and comfortable attire, such as polo shirts and light trousers, so they can maintain comfort without relying too heavily on air conditioning.

The "Cool Biz" campaign has been widely successful, resulting in significant energy savings and reduction in greenhouse gas emissions. By simply adjusting indoor temperatures and promoting sustainable dress codes, Tokyo has effectively mitigated the urban heat island effect and increased the resilience of its urban population to rising temperatures.

Case Study 3: Hima Approach in the Middle East

In the arid and semi-arid regions of the Middle East, climate change poses numerous challenges, including water scarcity and desertification. To combat these issues, an age-old nature conservation approach known as the Hima system has been successfully revived.

The Hima system involves the wise management of natural resources, particularly water and pasturelands, through the establishment of community-led protected areas. These areas are designated for sustainable use by local communities, who decide on regulations for grazing, cultivation, and sustainable water usage.

By reviving the Hima system, many Middle Eastern countries have successfully adapted to climate change by mitigating water scarcity and conserving their natural ecosystems. This bottom-up approach not only facilitates community resilience but also ensures the continuity and availability of vital resources in the face of climate uncertainty.

Overall, these case studies demonstrate that successful climate adaptation initiatives can be diverse and context-specific. Whether it's through innovative technologies like floating gardens, simple behavioral changes like the "Cool Biz" campaign, or traditional conservation approaches like the Hima system, the key lies in identifying and implementing strategies that empower communities to adapt and thrive in a changing climate.

Chapter 10: Role of Governments and Policies

In this chapter, we will dive into the crucial and multifaceted role that governments play in shaping economies and societies. We will explore various policies governments adopt to address economic challenges, promote growth, and ensure social welfare. From fiscal policy to labor market regulations, governments have extensive power to influence the direction and dynamics of their countries.

One of the fundamental roles of governments is macroeconomic management, which involves using fiscal and monetary policies to stabilize the economy. Fiscal policy refers to the use of government spending and taxation to influence the overall level of economic activity. Governments have the power to increase spending or cut taxes during downturns to stimulate growth and reduce unemployment. On the other hand, during periods of high inflation, governments may decrease spending or raise taxes to cool down the economy.

Monetary policy, on the other hand, is the responsibility of central banks. They manage the money supply, set interest rates, and regulate the banking sector. By manipulating interest rates, central banks can influence borrowing costs for businesses and individuals, thus impacting consumption and investment levels. Moreover, they have the authority to control the supply of money in the economy to maintain price stability and avoid excessive inflation or deflation.

Governments also implement industrial policies to promote specific sectors or regions within their countries. These policies can include providing subsidies, tax incentives, and infrastructure development for targeted industries. The goal is to boost economic growth, generate employment opportunities, and enhance competitiveness in international markets. However, the effectiveness of industrial policies remains a subject of debate, as governments need to carefully balance interventionism with market forces to avoid distorting resource allocation and creating inefficiencies.

Labor market regulations are another crucial aspect of government policies. They determine the conditions under which businesses can hire and fire employees, the minimum wage levels, and the rights and protections afforded to workers. Governments play a vital role in ensuring fair and equal treatment in the workplace and preventing exploitation. Striking the right balance between flexibility for employers and protection for employees is a delicate task, as overly rigid labor regulations can hinder job creation and economic mobility, while weak ones can allow for exploitation and erosion of workers' rights.

Furthermore, governments are responsible for promoting social welfare and addressing income inequalities. They have to implement redistributive policies such as progressive taxation, welfare programs, and social assistance. These measures aim to reduce poverty, ensure access to essential services like healthcare and education, and provide a safety net for vulnerable populations. Simultaneously, governments must foster an environment that encourages entrepreneurship and innovation, creating opportunities for upward social and economic mobility.

Globalization and international relations also heavily shape the role of governments and their policies. Governments often collaborate to coordinate economic policies, negotiate trade agreements, and establish global institutions for international cooperation. However, geopolitical tensions, protectionist policies, and disparities in economic development can hinder such collaborative efforts.

In conclusion, governments have a crucial role in shaping economies and societies through a wide array of policies. They maneuver fiscal and monetary policies to stabilize the economy, implement industrial policies to promote growth, regulate labor markets to ensure fairness, and pursue social welfare objectives. Balancing the interests of different stakeholders and addressing emerging global challenges is an ongoing task for governments worldwide.

- Evaluation of the role governments play in addressing global warming

The evaluation of the role governments play in addressing global warming is a complex and extensive topic. Governments have a crucial role to play in tackling this global challenge, as they possess the authority and resources needed to make the necessary policy changes and implement strategies to mitigate climate change and its impacts. In this evaluation, we will assess the actions taken by governments to address global warming, analyze their effectiveness, and explore potential areas for improvement.

Governments play a significant role in combating global warming through the formulation and implementation of policies aimed at reducing greenhouse gas emissions. One key policy tool employed by governments is the establishment of energy and environmental regulations. These regulations often include emission reduction targets, carbon pricing mechanisms, and incentives for renewable energy development. By setting mandatory emission standards, governments create a framework that encourages industries to adopt cleaner technologies and practices. Furthermore, the implementation of carbon pricing mechanisms, such as carbon taxes or emissions trading systems, provides economic incentives for businesses to reduce their carbon footprints.

Governments also play a leading role in international climate negotiations and agreements. The United Nations Framework Convention on Climate Change (UNFCCC) brings together world governments to address global warming collectively. One of the most notable outcomes of these negotiations is the Paris Agreement, reached in 2015. Governments can commit to specific emission reduction targets under this agreement and work collaboratively to limit the global temperature increase well below 2 degrees Celsius above pre-industrial levels. The Active Participation by governments in the Paris Agreement is crucial in ensuring collective efforts to combat global warming.

Furthermore, governments often invest in research and development initiatives to promote innovation in clean energy technologies. They provide funding for projects focused on renewable energy, energy efficiency, and carbon capture and storage. These investments stimulate technological advancements, reduce costs, and facilitate the transition to a low-carbon economy.

While governments have taken significant steps to address global warming, there are areas for improvement. One major challenge is the need for stronger enforcement of existing regulations and policies. Some governments may face political pressures or lack resources to effectively enforce emission reduction targets or adequately monitor environmental compliance. Thus, there is a need for increased monitoring, reporting, and verification mechanisms to ensure transparency and accountability in the implementation of climate policies.

Another area for improvement is the integration of climate change considerations into broader government policies and sectors. Climate change is a cross-cutting issue that can impact various sectors, including agriculture, transport, and industry. Governments need to adopt a holistic approach that incorporates climate change considerations into these sectors' policies, thus promoting sustainable practices and resilience.

Moreover, there is a need for greater international cooperation on climate change. While the Paris Agreement is a landmark agreement, some governments have been hesitant or reluctant to fulfill their commitments, creating uncertainties about the global efforts to combat global warming. Governments should strive for increased cooperation, knowledge-sharing, and support to developing countries in their climate change adaptation and mitigation efforts.

In conclusion, evaluating the role of governments in addressing global warming reveals both progress made and challenges ahead. Governments have established policies, regulations, and international agreements as critical tools in the fight against climate change. However, stronger enforcement, cross-sectoral integration, and enhanced international cooperation are necessary to drive sustainable progress. Governments must continue to prioritize climate action and work collectively to achieve a safe, sustainable, and resilient future for our planet.

- Discussion of effective policies and regulations at national and international levels

Effective policies and regulations are vital tools for governments to ensure the smooth operation of their countries and to address pressing issues such as economic growth, environmental protection, and social justice. These policies and regulations can be enacted at both national and international levels, taking into account the unique circumstances of each country while also promoting global cooperation and alignment of goals.

At the national level, governments have the responsibility to create an environment that promotes sustainable development, protects citizens' rights, and fosters economic prosperity. This requires a comprehensive set of policies and regulations that address a wide range of issues. For example, economic policies should aim to create a conducive business environment, promote innovation and entrepreneurship, and provide support to struggling sectors. Strong regulations are necessary to ensure fair competition, prevent market abuses, and protect both consumers and workers.

Environmental policies and regulations are crucial to address the challenges of climate change, pollution, and resource depletion. Governments must set ambitious targets for reducing greenhouse gas emissions, promote clean energy sources, and devise regulations that hold industries accountable for their environmental impacts. Incentives and subsidies can also be provided to promote sustainable practices and encourage investment in green technologies.

Social policies should aim to provide equal opportunities for all citizens, improve access to education and healthcare, and promote social cohesion. Regulations can be adopted to prevent discrimination, enforce labor rights, and eradicate poverty. Governments can also implement policies that reduce income inequality and promote wealth redistribution to ensure a fair and just society for all.

While national policies and regulations are essential, cooperation between countries is crucial to tackle global challenges that transcend borders. At the international level, organizations such as the United Nations, World Trade Organization, and International Monetary Fund play a vital role in setting global standards and facilitating dialogue between nations.

International agreements and treaties are key instruments for harmonizing policies and regulations across different countries. For example, the Paris Agreement on climate change aims to limit global warming to well below 2 degrees Celsius and foster financing and technological support for developing countries. Similarly, trade agreements seek to establish common rules and eliminate barriers to promote global commerce.

Efforts should be made to align national policies with international objectives and commitments. This requires coordination and cooperation among governments, as well as the sharing of best practices and knowledge. National policies must take into account global considerations to ensure that countries are not acting in isolation or undermining global efforts.

Furthermore, effective policies and regulations must be transparent, accountable, and adaptable. Governments should engage citizens and stakeholders in decision-making processes and ensure that policies are evidence-based, economically viable, and have clear objectives. Monitoring and evaluation mechanisms should be put in place to measure the effectiveness of policies and measure progress towards desired goals. Moreover, policies should be flexible enough to adapt to changing circumstances and emerging challenges.

In conclusion, effective policies and regulations at both national and international levels are essential mechanisms to address various issues and promote welfare. They must be comprehensive, transparent, and accountable, taking into account specific local contexts while promoting global cooperation and alignment of goals. By formulating and implementing effective policies and regulations, governments can steer their countries towards sustainable development, social justice, and a brighter future.

- Analysis of challenges faced by governments in implementing sustainable practices

Governments around the world are increasingly recognizing the need to implement sustainable practices in order to address environmental concerns and promote long-term economic and social development. However, the path to achieving sustainable goals is riddled with challenges that governments must navigate. In this analysis, we will delve into some of the major challenges faced by governments in implementing sustainable practices.

One significant challenge is the balancing act between short-term costs and long-term benefits. Sustainable practices often require substantial up-front investments, such as upgrading infrastructure or adopting new technologies. These costs can be a barrier for many governments facing tight budgets and urgent needs in other areas. Convincing taxpayers and policymakers of the long-term benefits and return on investment is crucial for governments to garner support for such investments.

Another challenge is the complexity and interconnectedness of sustainable practices. Implementing sustainability initiatives often requires coordination and collaboration across various government agencies, as well as stakeholders from the private sector and civil society. This necessitates effective governance structures that can facilitate integrated decision-making and overcome siloed approaches. Governments must invest in building capacity and promoting interdisciplinary collaborations to address these challenges.

Additionally, governments face challenges in creating an enabling policy framework for sustainable practices. Policies need to be ambitious, yet attainable and realistic. Striking the right balance between regulation and flexibility is crucial to promote sustainable practices without stifling economic growth. Governments must consider the unique context and socio-cultural factors to ensure policies are tailored to specific challenges and opportunities.

Funding is another major hurdle governments face. While sustainable practices may generate long-term economic benefits, securing adequate funding in the short term can be a challenge. Governments must explore innovative financing mechanisms, such as public-private partnerships, green bonds, or carbon pricing, to attract investment and leverage resources efficiently.

A key challenge that cannot be overlooked is the issue of social acceptance and behavior change. Sustainable practices often require changes in habits, consumption patterns, and lifestyles which can be met with resistance from the public. Governments must invest in education and awareness campaigns to promote understanding and acceptance of sustainable practices. Public participation and engagement are also critical in order to create grassroots ownership and support for sustainability initiatives.

Furthermore, governments face challenges in monitoring and evaluating their sustainability strategies. Robust monitoring mechanisms are necessary to track progress, identify gaps, and adapt strategies accordingly. Data collection, analysis, and reporting require adequate resources and capacity-building efforts to ensure accurate and relevant information.

Lastly, governments often face challenges in overcoming political and institutional barriers. Political will, leadership, and commitment to sustainability are crucial for driving change. However, governments may face resistance from vested interests, bureaucratic inertia, or short-term political pressures. Overcoming these barriers requires strategic communication, capacity-building, and stakeholder engagement to build consensus and create a supportive political environment for sustainable practices.

In conclusion, governments face numerous challenges in implementing sustainable practices. Balancing short-term costs and long-term benefits, creating an enabling policy framework, securing adequate funding, promoting behavior change, and overcoming institutional barriers are just a few of the hurdles that governments must address. Yet, despite these challenges, it is crucial for governments to prioritize sustainability in order to effectively address environmental concerns and promote sustainable development for the well-being of current and future generations.

Chapter 11: Public Awareness and Education

In today's world, where information is readily available at the touch of a button, it is crucial for organizations and individuals to harness the power of public awareness and education. Whether it is about critical issues such as health, environment, social justice, or any other arena, educating and creating awareness among the masses is essential for fostering positive change.

This chapter will delve into the significance of public awareness and education and provide valuable insights into how to effectively implement and maximize their impact.

1. Importance of Public Awareness and Education:

Public awareness and education play a vital role in shaping policies, behaviors, and attitudes. They empower individuals to make informed decisions and take actions that contribute to the betterment of society. By disseminating accurate and reliable information, public awareness campaigns bridge the gap between knowledge and action, mobilizing citizens to be proactive participants in various spheres.

2. Objectives of Public Awareness and Education:

a. Knowledge Dissemination: Public awareness and education aim to provide accurate, relevant, and timely information to the target audience. By doing so, they promote understanding, awareness, and consciousness about specific issues or causes.

b. Behavior Change: A key objective of public awareness and education is to bring about positive changes in attitudes, beliefs, and behaviors. By presenting compelling narratives and illustrating the direct consequences of certain actions, these campaigns aim to inspire behavioral shifts that align with societal or organizational objectives.

c. Proactive Engagement: Public awareness and education stimulate individuals to actively engage with the subject matter. By involving them in discussions, initiatives, and events, these campaigns encourage critical thinking, problem-solving, and participation in larger societal issues.

d. Advocacy and Support: An essential outcome of effective public awareness and education is the proliferation of advocacy efforts and support for particular causes. By raising public consciousness, they cultivate a sense of responsibility and empathy while empowering individuals to take action, contribute, and champion the causes they believe in.

3. Effective Strategies for Public Awareness and Education:

a. Understanding the Target Audience: To create an impact, it is crucial to identify the needs, values, and preferences of the target audience. Understanding their motivations and challenges will allow for tailored messaging and approaches that resonate with the audience and maximize engagement.

b. Utilizing Multiple Channels: In today's fast-paced digital era, it is essential to leverage a variety of communication channels including traditional media, social media, websites, and community outreach activities. This multi-channel approach ensures that the message reaches a diverse audience and facilitates active participation.

c. Providing Compelling Content: Captivating content is the backbone of any successful public awareness and education campaign. By employing storytelling techniques, impactful visuals, and relatable narratives, campaigns can capture attention, evoke emotions, and ultimately drive action.

d. Collaboration and Partnerships: Collaborating with organizations and individuals who share similar goals can amplify the impact of a public awareness campaign. By pooli

- Emphasizing the significance of public awareness and education in combating global warming

Public awareness and education are perhaps the most powerful tools we have at our disposal to combat global warming. With the urgency of the climate crisis becoming increasingly apparent, it is crucial that people understand the gravity of the situation and take action.

One of the main reasons why public awareness and education are so important is because global warming is a complex issue that requires everyone's understanding and effort. From understanding the causes of climate change to recognizing the potential solutions, educating the public can help mobilize individuals and communities to make sustainable choices. With a better understanding of the problem, people are more likely to support policies and participate in initiatives that reduce greenhouse gas emissions and mitigate the effects of climate change.

Moreover, public awareness and education can generate the political will needed to implement significant changes on a global scale. When citizens are well-informed about the impacts of global warming and the potential solutions, they are more likely to demand action from their governments and hold elected officials accountable for climate policies. By raising public consciousness, we create a sense of urgency that pushes governments to take necessary action, such as implementing clean energy regulations or investing in renewable technologies.

Furthermore, public awareness and education can foster behavioral change on an individual level. By understanding the environmental consequences of their actions, people are more likely to adopt sustainable behaviors in their daily lives. Whether it is reducing energy consumption, recycling, or choosing green transportation options, individual actions can have a cumulative effect and make a significant difference in reducing greenhouse gas emissions.

In addition, public awareness and education can also pave the way for innovation and technological advancements. When the public is informed about the threats and possibilities surrounding climate change, it sparks a desire for solutions. This fuels research and development in areas such as renewable energy, carbon capture technologies, and sustainable agriculture. By educating the public about the potential of these advancements, we create a demand for sustainable solutions and encourage further innovation.

It is important to note that public awareness and education should go beyond scientific knowledge alone. The communication of climate change should also acknowledge the economic, social, and political aspects of the issue. By framing the narrative in a way that resonates with diverse audiences, we can foster inclusivity and encourage wider engagement in climate action. This means tailoring educational campaigns to address the specific concerns and interests of different communities, emphasizing co-benefits such as job creation or public health improvements.

In summary, public awareness and education play a central role in combating global warming. They enable citizens to understand the gravity of the problem, build political will for action, foster behavioral change, encourage innovation, and promote inclusive climate action. By emphasizing the significance of public awareness and education, we can inspire a collective commitment to create a sustainable and livable future for generations to come.

- Examination of successful educational campaigns and their impact on behavior change

Examination of Successful Educational Campaigns and Their Impact on Behavior Change: A Comprehensive Analysis

Abstract:

In an ever-evolving world, education has taken center stage as an effective tool for promoting positive behavior change. Educational campaigns capitalize on the power of knowledge and information dissemination to influence attitudes, beliefs, and actions towards certain societal issues or personal habits. This article presents an in-depth examination of successful educational campaigns and their profound impact on behavior change. Through a systematic review of literature and evaluation of case studies, this study aims to uncover key strategies and elements that contribute to the success of such campaigns, shedding light on their immense potential for creating influential societal transformations.

SUCCESSFUL EDUCATIONAL campaigns play a pivotal role in shaping behavior change across diverse spheres, including health, environmental practices, road safety, financial management, and more. These campaigns leverage educational approaches to equip individuals with knowledge, inspire critical thinking, and ultimately drive sustained behavior change. By analyzing their methodologies, impact assessment frameworks, and core components, this examination aims to provide valuable insights for designing future educational campaigns more effectively.

I. Methodology:

To comprehensively understand the influence of educational campaigns, a systematic review of existing literature exploring successful campaigns conducted within the last decade has been crucial. Several renowned databases, including PubMed, Scopus, and Google Scholar, were consulted to identify peer-reviewed articles focusing on the outcomes of various educational campaigns. Qualitative assessment tools were employed to collect relevant data, prioritize campaigns, and assess their impact on behavior change. Additionally, relevant case studies were analyzed to provide real-world examples of successful educational campaigns and to illuminate critical success factors.

II. Impactful Behavior Change Strategies:

a. Engaging Multimedia:

Successful campaigns utilize visually compelling and interactive multimedia tools to capture audiences' attention and amplify the campaign's reach and impact. Engaging videos, immersive virtual reality experiences, interactive websites, and social media content are some of the key strategies employed in effective campaigns for behavior change.

b. Pioneering Messaging Approaches:

Campaign messages, whether through explicit content or subtle storytelling, need to engage with targeted audiences at an emotional level while highlighting influential incentives for behavior change. Deploying positive affirmation techniques, beyond fear appeals, has proven to be an effective emotional connection that incites desired actions.

c. Peer Influence and Role Models:

Highly impactful campaigns intentionally leverage peer networks and influential role models, utilizing collective norms and aspirations to foster behavior change. Relying on testimonials, testimonials from credible sources who have adopted the desired behavior further enhances the campaign's persuasive power.

d. Community-Based Approaches:

Educational campaigns that engage local communities have a significant impact on behavior change due to their targeted messaging and the creation of personal connections. By incorporating localized knowledge, culture, and methods of communication, campaigns inspire ownership among community members, resulting in sustainable behavior change.

III. Measuring Impact:

Campaign success heavily relies on rigorous evaluation, providing insights into the effectiveness and long-term impact of deployed strategies. Robust impact assessment frameworks, including surveys, behavioral observations, and measures of attitude change, must be incorporated to quantitatively identify behavioral transformations and improvements aligned with educational campaign goals.

IV. Case Study Analysis:

Several exemplary case studies, including anti-smoking campaigns, safe driving initiatives, and environmental awareness campaigns, were closely evaluated and dissected to illuminate the above strategies' successful utilization. In each case, unique aspects and approaches were identified, pointing towards an evolving and dynamic campaign landscape.

———●———

THE EXAMINATION AND analysis of successful educational campaigns and their impact on behavior change provide invaluable lessons for designing future interventions. Armed with this knowledge, policymakers, educators, and social influencers can create more effective campaigns capable of achieving substantial behavior change to address societal challenges and promote positive transformations in individuals' lives.

- Proposals for enhanced public engagement and achieving sustainable practices

Proposals for Enhanced Public Engagement and Achieving Sustainable Practices

ENHANCED PUBLIC ENGAGEMENT plays a crucial role in achieving sustainable practices. It is essential for government bodies, organizations, and communities to actively involve the public in decision-making processes related to sustainability goals. This article puts forth several proposals aimed at optimizing public engagement and fostering sustainable practices across various sectors.

Proposal 1: Public Participation Platforms

One effective way to enhance public engagement is through the development of user-friendly online platforms. These platforms can serve as a hub for citizens to provide input, exchange ideas, and participate in relevant discussions. Local government bodies can create specific sections on these platforms where different initiatives, policies, and projects related to sustainability are highlighted, thereby encouraging public participation. These platforms should also offer interactive features, such as survey tools, which enable community members to express their opinions easily.

Proposal 2: Empowering Community Organizations

Another crucial aspect of public engagement is empowering community organizations. Governments and businesses should collaborate with local community-based organizations that focus on sustainability. By providing resources, funding, and technical support, these organizations can effectively engage the public, mobilize volunteers, and develop localized sustainable solutions. Such partnerships can promote grassroots engagement and help create inclusive strategies.

Proposal 3: Education and Awareness Campaigns

Educational campaigns are fundamental in raising public awareness about sustainability practices. Governments, NGOs, and private companies should join forces to design robust campaigns that educate individuals about sustainable lifestyle choices, environmental issues, and the impact of specific practices. Schools can play a crucial role in integrating sustainability education into their curricula. Additionally, awareness campaigns utilizing various media platforms can significantly enhance knowledge dissemination and foster public engagement.

Proposal 4: Collaboration between Public and Private Sectors

Public-private partnerships are critical for driving sustainable practices. The government should actively engage with private sector actors to create incentives that encourage environmentally conscious practices. Companies can incorporate sustainable practices into their operations, commit to renewable energy usage, and support sustainable supply chains. In return, governments can offer tax breaks, subsidies, and assistance with regulatory compliance. Such collaborations can effectively combine the strengths and resources of both sectors toward achieving sustainable goals.

Proposal 5: Governance Transparency and Data Sharing

To enhance public engagement, transparent governance is vital. Governments and organizations should make sustainable practices more accessible by providing clear and concise information regarding their plans and progress. This can involve sharing reports, data, and real-time updates on sustainability initiatives. Publicly available data allows citizens to engage critically and hold policymakers accountable. The use of data visualization tools can also aid public understanding and support meaningful engagement.

Proposal 6: Inclusive Decision-Making Processes

Finally, ensuring inclusive decision-making processes is essential for enhanced public engagement. Governments should actively strive to include diverse voices, especially marginalized communities, in sustainable practice discussions. Efforts should be made to break down language barriers, provide accommodations, and make participation equitable and accessible to all. Additionally, fostering collaboration and public deliberation can help overcome conflicts and come up with innovative and sustainable solutions.

ENHANCED PUBLIC ENGAGEMENT is vital in achieving sustainable practices. By implementing the proposals discussed above, stakeholders can optimize public involvement and encourage the adoption of sustainable strategies. Only through inclusive and participatory decision-making can we work towards a more sustainable future for our communities and the planet.

Chapter 12: Corporate Responsibility and Innovation

In today's rapidly changing business landscape, the concept of corporate responsibility and innovation has gained significant importance. Companies across various industries are realizing that they need to adapt and respond to evolving societal and environmental challenges while also maintaining their competitive edge. This chapter provides a comprehensive analysis of corporate responsibility and its intersection with innovation.

Firstly, the chapter explores the fundamental concept of corporate responsibility. It dives into the definition and various dimensions of corporate responsibility, such as economic, social, and environmental responsibilities. It emphasizes the need for companies to not only focus on maximizing profits but also consider the impact their actions have on stakeholders and broader society. The chapter highlights how corporate responsibility is evolving from mere philanthropy to a more strategic and integrated approach within companies.

Furthermore, the chapter delves into the role of innovation in corporate responsibility. It illustrates how innovative approaches can help companies address societal and environmental challenges effectively. Innovation can play a vital role in finding sustainable alternatives to traditional business practices, reducing environmental impact, and creating value for a company and its stakeholders. The chapter provides real-life examples of companies embracing innovation to address issues like climate change, supply chain labor practices, and product safety.

One section of the chapter explores the concept of social innovation. It emphasizes the importance of collaboration between companies, governments, non-profit organizations, and communities in fostering social innovation. It highlights the role of cross-sector partnerships and co-creation in generating innovative solutions to tackle complex societal problems. The chapter showcases examples of companies engaging in social innovation initiatives to improve education, healthcare, and access to clean energy in underserved communities.

The chapter also addresses the growing expectations of stakeholders regarding corporate responsibility. It highlights the need for companies to be transparent in their actions, engage in dialogue with stakeholders, and incorporate their feedback in decision-making processes. It emphasizes the significance of measuring and reporting on corporate responsibility efforts to demonstrate accountability and progress. The chapter explores various frameworks and reporting standards that companies can adopt to enhance their corporate responsibility practices.

Lastly, the chapter discusses the potential challenges and barriers companies may face in implementing corporate responsibility and innovation initiatives. It acknowledges that pursuing corporate responsibility can sometimes require significant investments and a cultural shift within organizations. The chapter provides strategies and best practices for overcoming these challenges and outlines the business case for corporate responsibility and innovation.

Overall, this chapter presents a comprehensive overview of corporate responsibility and innovation. It sheds light on the evolving nature of corporate responsibility and emphasizes the crucial role of innovation for companies aiming to make a positive impact on society and the environment. With its thoughtful analysis and real-world examples, this chapter provides valuable insights for managers, professionals, and policymakers seeking to navigate the corporate responsibility landscape and drive meaningful change.

- Exploration of the role of corporations in addressing global warming

In recent years, global warming has become one of the most pressing issues that the world is facing. Its negative consequences have been observed and felt in various parts of the globe, from rising temperatures and melting ice caps to extreme weather events and the loss of biodiversity. In order to mitigate the impacts of this phenomenon, urgent action is required from all sectors of society, including governments, individuals, and corporations. This essay explores the role corporations can play in addressing global warming and highlights the importance of their involvement in tackling this global challenge.

Corporations, as some of the world's largest emitters of greenhouse gases (GHGs) and significant drivers of economic growth, have a crucial role to play in the fight against global warming. Through their operations and supply chains, corporations have the potential to implement and promote climate-friendly practices that can significantly reduce their carbon footprint. This can be achieved through various means, such as energy-efficient manufacturing processes, investment in renewable energy sources, and the development of sustainable business models.

One way corporations can address global warming is by actively reducing their greenhouse gas emissions. By implementing measures to increase energy efficiency, reducing waste, and adopting cleaner technologies, companies can significantly decrease their carbon emissions. This not only helps combat global warming but can also bring cost savings as energy efficiency often leads to reduced operational expenses. Leading corporations, such as Unilever and Apple, have set ambitious targets to become carbon neutral or use 100% renewable energy sources, thus showcasing their commitment to addressing global warming.

Alongside emissions reduction, another key area where corporations can make a substantial impact is by promoting sustainable practices throughout their supply chains. By engaging with suppliers and encouraging the adoption of eco-friendly processes, corporations can ensure that their entire value chain operates in an environmentally responsible manner. This can involve supporting suppliers to embrace renewable energy, encouraging the use of sustainable materials, and promoting ethical sourcing practices. Through their influence, corporations can help to drive sustainability beyond their own operations and extend their impact throughout the global economy.

Moreover, corporations have the power and resources to invest in research and development (R&D) efforts that can lead to groundbreaking technological advancements in the field of climate change mitigation. By funding innovation, corporations can contribute to the development of new technologies that promote renewable energy, enhance carbon capture and storage, and improve energy efficiency. These developments, if successfully implemented, could produce significant results in curbing global warming while revolutionizing industries for a more sustainable future.

Another important aspect of corporate involvement in addressing global warming lies in the realm of advocacy and policy support. Corporations can use their influence to promote policies that favor climate action and the adoption of regulations to reduce carbon emissions. By aligning business interests with climate action and advocating for stricter environmental standards, corporations can both contribute to the fight against global warming and create a level playing field for the entire business community. This active engagement in policy discussions can further incentivize governments worldwide to adopt ambitious climate targets and encourage broader international cooperation in tackling this shared challenge.

Furthermore, corporations can play a crucial role in mobilizing financial resources towards climate action. The transition to a low-carbon economy requires substantial investments in renewable energy infrastructure, research and development, and adaptation measures. Through sustainable finance and responsible investment practices, corporations can contribute funding to and support the development of projects and initiatives aimed at addressing global warming. This could involve providing financial assistance to start-ups in the clean energy sector, issuing green bonds, or allocating funds for the restoration of ecosystems. By leveraging their financial resources, corporations can accelerate the transition to a more sustainable and climate-resilient future.

However, it is noteworthy that not all corporations have adequately recognized the urgency of addressing global warming. Some may continue to prioritize profit maximization over sustainability goals, resulting in reinforcing the negative impacts associated with their operations. Addressing this challenge necessitates the establishment of clear regulatory frameworks and international standards for corporate sustainability and responsible behavior. Moreover, stakeholders across society should demand transparency and hold corporations accountable for their environmental impact. By applying pressure and incentivizing corporate sustainability measures, it becomes more likely that businesses will recognize the importance of taking action on global warming.

In conclusion, corporations have a critical role to play in addressing global warming. With their economic power, influence, expertise, and potential for technology and innovation, corporations have the capacity to drive change at a scale that can make a significant impact. By actively reducing their own emissions, promoting sustainability throughout supply chains, investing in R&D, advocating for climate policies, and mobilizing finance, corporations can be an important force in combating global warming. However, this requires a mindset shift towards prioritizing sustainability alongside profitability and the establishment of robust frameworks that incentivize corporate action. Only through collective efforts and collaborations between governments, individuals, and corporations, can we hope to effectively address the challenges of global warming and create a sustainable future for generations to come.

- Evaluation of sustainable business practices and corporate social responsibility

Evaluation of sustainable business practices and corporate social responsibility is an essential task for organizations in today's environmentally conscious and socially aware world. This evaluation involves assessing and analyzing various factors that impact sustainability and social responsibility within a company, including its environmental impact, ethical practices, employee welfare, community engagement, and global supply chain management. By conducting a comprehensive evaluation, organizations can gauge their performance in these areas, identify areas for improvement, and develop strategies to enhance their sustainability and social responsibility practices.

One of the key aspects of evaluating sustainable business practices and corporate social responsibility is examining a company's environmental impact. This involves analyzing the company's carbon footprint, energy consumption, waste management, and use of natural resources. By assessing these factors, organizations can identify opportunities to reduce their environmental impact and adopt sustainable practices, such as implementing energy-efficient processes, reducing waste generation, and promoting the use of renewable energy. Moreover, by setting measurable targets and tracking progress, companies can continuously improve their environmental performance.

Ethical practices are another crucial area that should be evaluated in terms of sustainable business practices and corporate social responsibility. This involves examining the transparency, fairness, and integrity of a company's operations. Organizations need to ensure that their supply chain practices adhere to ethical sourcing guidelines, respect human rights, and promote fair trade practices. By regularly monitoring and assessing suppliers' conformity with these standards, companies can minimize the risk of unethical practices, such as forced labor, child labor, and environmental exploitation.

Employee welfare is also an integral part of evaluating sustainable business practices and corporate social responsibility. This includes assessing the organization's commitment to providing a safe and healthy work environment, fostering diversity and inclusion, promoting employee development, and ensuring appropriate work-life balance. By conducting regular employee satisfaction surveys, organizations can gauge the effectiveness of their efforts in these areas and identify potential areas for improvement. Additionally, providing competitive wages and benefits, encouraging employee engagement, and supporting employee well-being can contribute to a positive work environment and enhance the organization's reputation as a socially responsible employer.

Community engagement and philanthropy play an essential role in evaluating sustainable business practices and corporate social responsibility. Companies need to understand the impact their operations have on local communities and identify opportunities to contribute positively. This can range from supporting local charities and non-profit organizations to investing in community development projects or volunteering initiatives. By creating meaningful partnerships and engaging with stakeholders, businesses can build trust and promote sustainable economic development in the communities they operate in.

Global supply chain management is another critical area when evaluating sustainable business practices and corporate social responsibility. Companies need to ensure that their suppliers follow ethical and sustainable practices throughout the supply chain. This includes promoting responsible sourcing, avoiding suppliers involved in unethical practices, and encouraging supplier diversity. Companies can assess the sustainability performance of their suppliers through audits, certifications, and supplier scorecards, ensuring they align with the organization's sustainability objectives.

In conclusion, the evaluation of sustainable business practices and corporate social responsibility involves examining various aspects such as environmental impact, ethical practices, employee welfare, community engagement, and global supply chain management. By thoroughly assessing these factors, organizations can identify areas for improvement, develop strategies to enhance their sustainability and social responsibility practices, and contribute to a more inclusive and sustainable future.

- Highlighting successful case studies of innovative companies contributing to mitigation efforts

S uccess Stories: Innovative Companies Paving the Way for Environmental Mitigation

IN TODAY'S WORLD, WHERE climate change and environmental degradation pose significant threats, it has become imperative for companies to take an active role in mitigating their impact on the planet. Thankfully, a new generation of innovative companies has risen to the occasion, combining sustainable business practices with cutting-edge technologies to drive positive environmental change. In this article, we present a series of success stories showcasing companies that have gone above and beyond, leading the charge towards a more sustainable future.

1. Tesla- Accelerating the Electric Vehicle Revolution:

Tesla, led by visionary Elon Musk, has revolutionized the automotive industry through its high-performance electric vehicles (EVs). By producing sleek, appealing cars that offer optimal driving experience without carbon emissions, Tesla has redefined the concept of clean transportation. The company's success has bolstered the adoption of EVs, with traditional automakers now investing heavily in sustainable technologies. Tesla's contribution to mitigating climate change by reducing vehicle carbon emissions has been remarkable.

2. Patagonia- Rewriting the Rulebook on Sustainability:

Patagonia, an outdoor apparel company, has been a pioneer of sustainable fashion for decades. From using recycled materials in their products to reducing water consumption throughout the manufacturing process, Patagonia sets an impressive sustainability benchmark. Furthermore, the company actively advocates for environmental causes and donates a substantial portion of its profits to support organizations working towards environmental protection. Patagonia's commitment to sustainable practices drives positive change within both the apparel industry and the communities it serves.

3. Enphase Energy- Empowering Clean Energy Solutions:

Enphase Energy, a prominent supporter of renewable energy, has developed intelligent solar microinverters. These devices maximize energy output and simplifies solar power installations, making them increasingly accessible for residential and commercial use. By optimizing energy production and improving overall system efficiency, Enphase Energy helps reduce the reliance on fossil fuels and encourages a transition to sustainable energy sources. The company's efforts contribute significantly to curbing greenhouse gas emissions.

4. Seventh Generation- Promoting Naturally Responsible Choices:

Seventh Generation, a leading brand in eco-friendly household products, commits to using plant-based ingredients and minimizing the environmental impact of its products. Through sustainable sourcing, waste reduction, and innovative product designs, Seventh Generation promotes a greener lifestyle. The company's transparency and commitment to both social and environmental values serve as an inspiration for other businesses striving to make positive changes on a global scale.

5. Interface Inc.- Redefining Sustainable Flooring:

Interface Inc., a flooring company, has been a sustainability champion in the construction industry. By implementing new manufacturing processes and adhering to strict material sourcing standards, Interface has successfully reduced its carbon footprint. The company has set ambitious goals, such as its "Mission Zero" initiative, focused on eliminating any negative environmental impact by 2020. Interface's dedication to innovation, sustainability, and environmental stewardship highlights the potential for transformation in traditionally resource-intensive sectors.

⸺⸺◉⸺⸺

THE SUCCESS STORIES of companies like Tesla, Patagonia, Enphase Energy, Seventh Generation, and Interface Inc. demonstrate that businesses can play a pivotal role in mitigation efforts. These innovative companies highlight the possibilities for positive environmental change through sustainable practices, renewable energy solutions, and conscious consumer choices. As we look forward, inspiring examples from these and many other innovative companies indicate that a brighter, greener future is not only desirable but achievable.

Chapter 13: Social Equity and Environmental Justice

In recent years, the concept of environmental justice has gained increasing attention. Environmental justice focuses on the fair distribution of environmental burdens and benefits among different social groups. It strives to address the unequal environmental conditions and challenges faced by marginalized communities, ensuring that all individuals have the opportunity to live in a healthy and safe environment. This chapter delves into the multifaceted dynamics of social equity and environmental justice, exploring their intricacies, importance, and the actions required to achieve them.

Unequal Environmental Conditions:

Social inequities are often intertwined with environmental disparities. Low-income communities and communities of color, in many instances, bear the burden of environmental threats such as pollution, toxic waste sites, and inadequate access to clean water and air. These vulnerable communities often lack political power and are unable to influence decision-making processes. As a result, they face disproportionate environmental risks, compromising their rights to health and an acceptable quality of life.

Historical Context:

The roots of environmental justice can be traced back to various historic events and social movements that aimed to challenge discrimination and inequities. In the United States, for instance, the civil rights movement played a vital role in laying the foundations for environmental justice activism. In the 1980s, prominent incidents like the Love Canal and Warren County protests highlighted how marginalized communities were disproportionately affected by hazardous waste disposal and toxic pollution. These events served as catalysts for the emergence of the environmental justice movement.

Environmental Racism:

Environmental racism refers to the practice of intentionally placing environmentally harmful facilities, such as landfills and chemical plants, in communities predominantly inhabited by diverse minority groups. This discriminatory practice further exacerbates existing social inequities, perpetuating the concentration of environmental risks in already marginalized communities. The detrimental health impacts resulting from environmental racism can be severe and long-lasting.

Impacts on Public Health:

The unequal distribution of environmental hazards significantly affects public health outcomes. Exposure to air and water pollution, hazardous substances, and contaminated environments increases the risk of various health problems, including respiratory illnesses, cancer, and developmental disorders. Vulnerable populations, such as children, the elderly, and individuals with pre-existing health conditions, face heightened susceptibility to these adverse health effects.

Policy and Advocacy:

Efforts to address social equity and environmental justice involve policy changes, community advocacy, and legal action. Policymakers play a crucial role in creating regulations that ensure the equitable distribution of environmental resources and discourage environmental discrimination. Grassroots organizations and community activists have been instrumental in mobilizing impacted communities, raising awareness, and demanding justice.

Promoting Social Equity:

Achieving social equity and environmental justice requires systemic changes and the involvement of numerous stakeholders. Implementing environmental justice principles in decision-making processes, such as conducting robust environmental impact assessments, promoting community engagement, and ensuring equal representation, can lead to more just and equitable outcomes. Additionally, addressing underlying social determinants of environmental injustices, including income inequality, access to healthcare and education, and affordable housing, is essential for making lasting progress.

⸻ ◉ ⸻

RECOGNIZING AND ADDRESSING social inequities and environmental injustices are imperative for building sustainable, resilient, and just societies. By placing social equity at the forefront of environmental decision-making processes, we can create a future where all individuals, regardless of their background, have equal access to clean and healthy environments. Environmental justice is not only a matter of fairness; it is an essential step towards a more inclusive and sustainable world.

- Analysis of the disproportionate impacts of global warming on vulnerable populations

Analysis of the Disproportionate Impacts of Global Warming on Vulnerable Populations

GLOBAL WARMING IS AN escalating problem with far-reaching consequences. While its effects are felt globally, certain segments of society are more vulnerable to its repercussions than others. This analysis aims to explore the disproportionate impacts of global warming on vulnerable populations, highlighting the intricate relationship between climate change and social inequalities.

Threatened Regions:

Several regions are highly susceptible to the impacts of global warming. Low-lying coastal areas exposed to rising sea levels often house vulnerable populations, including low-income communities and marginalized minorities. The Pacific Islands, Bangladesh, and parts of Africa, for example, face significant threats from climate-induced disasters such as deadly storms, flooding, and coastal erosion. Displacement and loss of livelihood mainly affect impoverished populations lacking financial resources to adapt or recover.

Extreme Weather Events:

With global warming, the frequency and severity of extreme weather events are on the rise. These events, including hurricanes, floods, heatwaves, and droughts, have devastating consequences for vulnerable communities. Limited infrastructure, inadequate disaster preparedness, and economic instability compound the hardships faced by marginalized groups during and after such events. Moreover, vulnerable populations often lack access to physical and mental healthcare resources crucial for recovery.

Food Security and Agriculture:

Global warming deeply affects agricultural practices and food security, disproportionately impacting vulnerable populations. Impacted regions face challenges linked to changes in rainfall patterns, crop failures, and shrinking ecosystems. Small-scale farmers and indigenous communities relying on subsistence farming find themselves teetering on the brink of survival.

Water Scarcity and Health:

Rising temperatures exacerbate issues related to water scarcity, primarily afflicting poverty-stricken communities. Access to clean water and sanitation facilities becomes precarious in regions hit by droughts or changing precipitation patterns. Consequently, vulnerable people suffer from waterborne diseases, poor hygiene, and inadequate sanitation infrastructures, leading to debilitating health outcomes.

Public Health:

Global warming significantly impacts public health, yet vulnerable populations bear the brunt of these consequences. Extreme heat threatens vulnerable communities, particularly the elderly, infants, and those with pre-existing health conditions. Respiratory illnesses worsen due to increased air pollution linked to climate change. Additionally, insect-borne diseases, such as malaria and dengue fever, become more prevalent as the range and prevalence of disease vectors expand.

Displacement and Forced Migration:

As climate change renders certain regions uninhabitable, vulnerable populations face the harrowing consequences of displacement and forced migration. As marginalized communities are driven out of their homes due to environmental degradation, conflict over resources and limited capacity for adaptation, they often become internally displaced people or refugees. This pattern not only further undermines the socio-economic fabric but also places additional strain on the limited resources of host communities.

Conclusions:

Global warming's disproportionate impacts on vulnerable populations emphasize the urgent need for climate action and addressing social inequalities. Recognizing these unjust outcomes is crucial for the formulation of policies that not only tackle climate change but also prioritize the needs and rights of marginalized communities. Collaboration between governments, international organizations, and local communities is essential to ensure the protection, resilience, and empowerment of vulnerable populations in the face of global warming.

115

- Examination of the concept of environmental injustice and its connection to global warming

Examination of the concept of environmental injustice and its connection to global warming

ENVIRONMENTAL INJUSTICE refers to the unequal distribution of environmental benefits and burdens based on race, socioeconomic status, and other factors. It encompasses the idea that marginalized and disadvantaged communities often experience a disproportionate share of environmental hazards and pollutants. When considering the concept of environmental justice, it is crucial to understand its connection to global warming, as both issues are intertwined and exacerbate one another. This article will delve into the various aspects of environmental injustice and its relationship with global warming, shedding light on the significance of addressing these issues collectively.

Disproportionate environmental burdens on marginalized communities:

Marginalized communities, especially those consisting of people of color and low-income individuals, often live in areas that bear the brunt of environmental hazards. These areas are characterized by a high prevalence of polluting industries, waste disposal sites, and other sources of pollution. This results in increased exposure to harmful substances such as air and water pollution, toxins, and hazardous wastes. Consequently, individuals residing in these communities face higher risks of developing health problems such as asthma, cancer, and respiratory illnesses.

Inadequate access to environmental resources:

Compounding the issue of disproportionate environmental burdens is the lack of access to environmental resources in marginalized communities. These communities tend to have fewer parks, green spaces, and clean water sources, limiting residents' opportunities for recreation, relaxation, and healthier lifestyles. With fewer green spaces and more concrete-dominated areas, these communities are also more susceptible to heat island effects, exacerbating the impact of global warming on their living conditions.

Climate change impacts and vulnerabilities:

Global warming intensifies the challenges faced by marginalized communities by amplifying climate change impacts and exacerbating existing vulnerabilities. The increased frequency and intensity of extreme weather events such as hurricanes, wildfires, and floods disproportionately affect these communities due to their limited adaptive capacity and resources. Consequently, marginalized groups face higher risks of displacement, property damage, and loss of livelihoods.

The role of systemic inequalities:

To understand why environmental injustice persists, it is crucial to analyze the underlying systemic inequalities that contribute to the issue. Historical and ongoing segregation, discriminatory practices, and uneven distribution of resources have perpetuated environmental inequalities. These systemic inequalities are reinforced by policies and regulations that often favor powerful industries and fail to adequately protect marginalized communities. As a result, these communities face higher barriers in participating in decision-making processes and advocating for their environmental rights.

Addressing environmental injustice and combating global warming:

It is imperative to recognize that addressing environmental injustice is a critical component of any effective strategy to combat global warming. Adopting a comprehensive approach that recognizes the intersectionality of these issues is essential. Key steps include:

1. Advancing environmental justice policies and legislation: Implementing policies that prioritize equitable distribution of environmental resources, address pollution hotspots, and protect vulnerable communities helps mitigate environmental injustices.

2. Empowering marginalized communities: Providing affected communities with the tools and resources needed to advocate for their own rights and participate in decision-making processes that impact their environment is crucial. It is essential to support community-led initiatives and ensure their access to equitable funding and support.

3. Promoting sustainable and equitable development: Promoting renewable energy, sustainable urban planning, green infrastructure, and resilient communities can support both climate action and environmental justice. It is vital to involve all stakeholders, including marginalized communities, in the planning and implementation of such initiatives.

4. Dismantling systemic inequalities: Addressing the root causes of environmental injustice necessitates tackling systemic racism, poverty, and other structural inequalities. This involves engaging in critical conversations, reshaping policies, and challenging discriminatory practices.

***

ENVIRONMENTAL INJUSTICE and global warming are interconnected challenges that require urgent attention and comprehensive action. By understanding the disproportionate burdens faced by marginalized communities and the systemic inequalities that perpetuate these disparities, we can champion environmental justice as an integral part of addressing global warming. Transformative change is needed at all levels, from policy development to grassroots activism, to foster a more sustainable, equitable, and climate-resilient future for all.

- Proposal of strategies to ensure social equity and justice in climate action efforts

Proposal of Strategies to Ensure Social Equity and Justice in Climate Action Efforts

ADDRESSING CLIMATE change requires global collaboration and a comprehensive approach that includes all segments of society. However, historically, climate action plans have often overlooked social equity and justice concerns, leading to disproportional impacts on marginalized communities. This proposal aims to outline strategies to ensure social equity and justice in climate action efforts, offering a fair and inclusive path towards a sustainable future.

1. Collaboration and Inclusive Decision-Making:

To ensure social equity and justice in climate action, meaningful inclusion and participation of all stakeholders is crucial. Decision-making processes should include representatives from marginalized communities, indigenous groups, civil society organizations, and advocacy groups. Collaboration should be encouraged throughout the planning, implementation, and evaluation of climate action initiatives to ensure diverse perspectives are incorporated.

2. Promote Environmental Justice:

Combatting climate change must also address the environmental inequalities faced by marginalized communities. Historically burdened communities facing higher pollution levels and fewer green spaces should be prioritized in climate action efforts. Addressing environmental justice entails identifying and mitigating disproportionate impacts, providing access to clean energy alternatives, strengthening local environmental enforcement, and investing in sustainable infrastructure in marginalized neighborhoods.

3. Economic and Social Support:

Climate action plans should integrate strategies that protect vulnerable populations from potential economic and social disadvantages. Adequate support mechanisms, such as job training, financial assistance, and skill development programs, can empower individuals in transitioning towards green industries. Additionally, social safety nets should be expanded to ensure communities do not bear the brunt of economic hardship resulting from efforts to mitigate climate change.

4. Education and Awareness:

Promoting awareness about climate change and its impact on social equity is crucial to ensure equitable action. Education programs should be developed to inform communities about their vulnerability to climate risks and empower them to actively participate in climate mitigation efforts. Raising awareness of sustainable practices, energy conservation, and adaptation strategies can also foster behavioral change at an individual and community level.

5. Data Collection and Monitoring:

Transparent and accurate data collection is essential to identify and address social inequities in climate action. Governments, organizations, and institutions involved in climate action must collect and publish data on climate-related vulnerabilities, access to resources, and implementation progress among different communities. Regular monitoring will allow for course corrections and reinforce accountability, ensuring that social equity and justice considerations remain integral to climate action efforts.

6. Partnerships and Investment:

Collaboration and financial investments are key for social equity and justice-oriented climate action. Governments, private sector entities, and international organizations need to prioritize funding toward initiatives that promote inclusive participation, technological innovation, and equitable governance. Public-private partnerships should be established to leverage expertise and resources from various sectors and ensure that climate justice remains a central tenet of all sustainability initiatives.

⎯⎯⎯◉⎯⎯⎯

INCORPORATING STRATEGIES that emphasize social equity and justice in climate action efforts is essential to promote inclusive and sustainable development. By prioritizing collaboration, environmental justice, economic support, education, data collection, and partnerships, we can strive towards a fair and equitable transition to a carbon-neutral future. Working together, we can ensure that all members of society have equal opportunities to thrive and contribute to a more sustainable planet.

Chapter 14: Future Challenges and Risks

In this chapter, we will explore the potential challenges and risks that lie ahead in our ever-changing world. As we look to the future, it is essential to consider the various factors that may impact our lives, our societies, and our planet. From technological advancements to global issues, let us delve into the intricacies and implications of these future challenges.

1. Technological Advancements:

One of the most significant challenges of the future lies in the rapid advancements in technology. While these developments have led to incredible progress and innovation, they also pose several risks. Artificial intelligence, for example, may disrupt industries and eliminate job opportunities, causing economic instability for many. Moreover, privacy concerns arise with the increasing reliance on digital platforms and interconnected devices. Striking a balance between technological advancement and maintaining ethical, equitable, and sustainable practices will be crucial.

2. Climate Change and Environmental Risks:

Climate change continues to be an imminent threat to our planet. Rising global temperatures, extreme weather events, and diminishing natural resources pose significant challenges. Mitigating and adapting to climate change will require collective efforts at the global, national, and individual levels. Sustainable practices, renewable energy initiatives, and conservation efforts are critical in safeguarding our environment for future generations.

3. Social and Cultural Challenges:

As societies evolve, new social and cultural challenges emerge. Globalization has connected people from various backgrounds and cultures, fostering diversity and multiculturalism. However, it also brings its own set of challenges, including the potential for cultural clashes and tensions. Navigating these differences while promoting inclusivity and understanding will be necessary to ensure peaceful coexistence and social harmony.

4. Economic Disparities and Inequality:

Although the world has made progress in reducing poverty and improving living standards, economic disparities and inequalities persist. The future will require addressing wealth gaps, ensuring fair access to resources and opportunities, and tackling systemic issues that perpetuate inequality. A robust social and economic infrastructure will be pivotal in ensuring a more equitable and sustainable future for all.

5. Healthcare and Public Health Challenges:

Advancements in healthcare have revolutionized medical treatments and improved life expectancy. However, new and emerging challenges demand our attention. Pandemics and infectious diseases pose significant risks to global health security. Ensuring accessible and affordable healthcare for all, strengthening public health infrastructure, and promoting preventive measures will be crucial in tackling these future challenges.

6. Governance and Political Risks:

Effective governance and political stability are vital for the smooth functioning of societies. However, political risks continue to be a prevalent concern in many parts of the world. Conflicts, corruption, inadequate governance, and ideological divisions can impede progress and stability. Nurturing transparency, accountability, and strong leadership will be essential for addressing these challenges and safeguarding our democratic values.

⎯⎯⎯◉⎯⎯⎯

AS WE NAVIGATE THE complexities and uncertainties of the future, it is crucial to proactively address the challenges and risks that lie ahead. However, it is not all doom and gloom. By recognizing these challenges, we open doors to opportunities for innovation, collaboration, and positive change. Through collective efforts, informed decision-making, and sustainable practices, we can shape a better future for ourselves and generations to come. Let us embrace these challenges as catalysts for growth and work towards building a more resilient, inclusive, and sustainable world.

- Discussion of the potential risks and challenges associated with addressing global warming

Global warming is one of the most pressing issues facing our planet today. Rising temperatures, melting ice caps, and extreme weather events are just some of the visible consequences of this phenomenon. As governments, scientists, and organizations worldwide scramble to find solutions and implement mitigation measures, it is crucial to acknowledge and discuss the potential risks and challenges associated with addressing global warming.

One of the primary risks of addressing global warming is the economic impact. Transitioning to cleaner and greener technologies often requires significant financial investments. Governments, businesses, and individuals must all bear these costs, which can be substantial in the short term. Additionally, certain industries heavily dependent on fossil fuels may suffer as a result of the transition, leading to potential job losses and economic disruptions.

Furthermore, global warming is a global issue that requires collective action. Countries around the world must come together, set aside political differences, and commit to reducing greenhouse gas emissions. However, achieving global cooperation and consensus on the best course of action is incredibly challenging. The need for equitable distribution of responsibilities and resources often sparks disagreements and hinders progress.

Addressing global warming also puts pressure on developing countries. Many of these nations are still striving to meet their basic human needs and develop sustainable economies. Transitioning away from fossil fuels can be more difficult for these countries due to limited resources, technology, and infrastructure. The burden of prioritizing climate goals while addressing development needs remains a significant challenge.

Additionally, addressing global warming requires changing societal behavior and consumption patterns. This can be met with resistance and skepticism from people who are unwilling to modify their habits. Overcoming the cultural and behavioral barriers to sustainable practices requires education, awareness, and long-term commitment.

Another challenge associated with addressing global warming is the uncertainty around the effectiveness of various mitigation measures. While reducing greenhouse gas emissions is a priority, the impact of these actions on climate change is not always clear-cut. Simulation models, indirect effects, and complex interactions make it difficult to predict the full extent of a policy or measure's efficacy. It is essential to balance short-term results with long-term sustainability to avoid unintended consequences or wasted efforts.

Finally, it is crucial to consider the potential unintended effects of some mitigation measures. For example, large-scale deployment of renewable energy technologies can lead to habitat destruction, displacement of local communities, or adverse environmental impacts. Striking a balance between addressing global warming and minimizing other ecological or social issues can be complicated and requires careful planning and execution.

In conclusion, while urgent action is indeed needed to address global warming, it is crucial to acknowledge and discuss the potential risks and challenges associated with these actions. Economic impacts, global cooperation, development priorities, societal resistance, uncertainty, and unintended consequences are some of the key concerns. Tackling these challenges requires collaborative and adaptive approaches that consider various aspects of human well-being and environmental sustainability.

- Analysis of possible detrimental consequences if action is not taken promptly

If action is not taken promptly and appropriately, there could be a range of detrimental consequences that may come into play. These consequences can have both immediate and long-term effects, impacting various aspects of our lives.

One possible detrimental consequence of inaction is the worsening of an already existing problem. In many cases, issues tend to persist and even escalate if left unaddressed. For instance, if corrective action is not taken to mitigate climate change, the rate at which temperatures rise and extreme weather events occur could increase exponentially. This could lead to more frequent natural disasters, loss of biodiversity, and disruptions to ecosystems, ultimately putting human lives and livelihoods at risk.

Inaction can also result in missed opportunities. Time is of the essence when it comes to problem-solving and making critical decisions. If action is delayed, valuable opportunities for growth, innovation, and development may disappear. For example, if a company fails to adapt to changing market trends and technological advancements, they may lose their competitive edge, potentially leading to decreased profits and market share.

Furthermore, the longer action is postponed, the more difficult and expensive it becomes to rectify the situation. Take public health crises like pandemics as an example. Delaying necessary measures, such as implementing quarantine measures or providing urgent medical assistance, can allow diseases to spread rapidly, making containment and eradication much more challenging. This could result in increased mortality rates and healthcare costs.

Inaction can also have societal repercussions. When pressing problems are not addressed in a timely manner, they can lead to social unrest and instability. For instance, if social and economic inequalities are not tackled with urgency, they can give rise to unrest, protests, and even social conflicts. This, in turn, can disrupt social cohesion, trust, and overall community well-being.

Furthermore, neglecting to take prompt action can have adverse effects on the environment. For example, if pollution levels are not adequately controlled or if sustainable practices are not adopted, the resulting damage can be irreversible. Biodiversity loss, deforestation, and soil erosion are just a few examples of the consequences that can arise from failing to take ecologically responsible actions.

Lastly, inaction can have adverse psychological impacts on individuals and communities. When people perceive that their concerns are being ignored or that nothing is being done to address their needs, feelings of frustration, anger, and helplessness can emerge. This can lead to decreased trust in institutions, polarization, and a general sense of resignation, potentially further exacerbating societal divisions.

In conclusion, the consequences of not taking prompt and appropriate action can reverberate through virtually every aspect of our lives. The worsening of existing problems, missed opportunities, increased difficulty in resolving issues, societal repercussions, environmental damage, and psychological impacts are all possible detrimental consequences that should be taken seriously. It is imperative that we act swiftly and decisively when faced with challenges to mitigate these potential negative outcomes.

- Exploration of potential unforeseen consequences of implementing certain mitigation measures

There are many potential unforeseen consequences that can arise when implementing certain mitigation measures, particularly in the context of policy-making and decision-making processes. While these measures are often designed to address particular issues or challenges, they can inadvertently give rise to unintended effects that may have long-lasting impacts. This exploration seeks to shed light on some of these consequences and highlight the complexity involved in implementing mitigation measures.

One such consequence is the potential for displacement of problems. When a mitigation measure is put in place to address one issue, it can sometimes inadvertently shift the problem to another area or population. For example, implementing stricter emission controls on vehicles in a major city may result in an increase in the number of vehicles being driven outside the city limits, thus causing an accumulation of pollution in surrounding rural areas. This can create new challenges for these communities and possibly worsen the overall environmental situation.

Another consequence to consider is the potential for negative reactions from affected stakeholders. When policies or measures are implemented without thorough consultation or consideration for the needs and concerns of all involved parties, there may be a backlash that could hinder the overall effectiveness of the intended mitigation efforts. This requires policymakers to engage in comprehensive stakeholder engagement processes to better understand the possible consequences and incorporate diverse perspectives into their decision-making.

Furthermore, there may be unintended social and economic effects when implementing mitigation measures. For example, imposing stricter regulations on industries to reduce their environmental impact may lead to job losses or shifts in economic activities, potentially causing economic hardship for affected individuals and communities. These consequences need to be considered and accounted for during the policy design to ensure that mitigation efforts do not compound social inequalities or inadvertently harm vulnerable populations.

Additionally, there can be behavioral and systemic responses that offset the intended impacts of mitigation measures. People and corporations may adapt to the new policies in ways that undermine their effectiveness. For instance, individuals may find alternative means to engage in the same emissions-generating activities or adopt wasteful practices elsewhere to compensate for the reduced impact in one area. This calls for continuous monitoring and evaluation of the implemented measures to ensure that they deliver the desired outcomes and do not foster unintended behavior changes.

In some cases, the implementation of mitigation measures can lead to burdensome compliance requirements or complex bureaucratic procedures. This can create significant barriers for businesses, especially small and medium-sized enterprises, and divert scarce resources towards compliance rather than meaningful environmental or social impact. Policymakers need to strike a balance between the desired progress and the practical implementation of measures to prevent stifling innovation or unduly burdening those they seek to regulate.

Finally, it is crucial to highlight the potential ethical considerations that can emerge as a result of implementing mitigation measures. Ethical dilemmas may arise concerning matters such as power dynamics, procedural justice, and allocation of resources. For example, questions can arise about the fairness of measuring and distributing environmental costs and benefits, with historically marginalized populations potentially suffering disproportionately from adverse consequences. As mitigation measures are devised, it becomes essential to actively consider and address these ethical implications to ensure equitable distribution of burdens and benefits.

In conclusion, while implementing mitigation measures is crucial to address challenges and achieve the desired outcomes, careful consideration of potential unforeseen consequences is paramount. The complexity involved necessitates thorough analysis, stakeholder engagement, monitoring, and decision-making that balance effectiveness and unintended harm. By recognizing and exploring these potential consequences, policymakers can be better prepared to anticipate challenges and adapt their approaches, ultimately contributing to more robust, sustainable, and informed decision-making processes.

Chapter 15: Outlook on the Future

As we near the end of this comprehensive journey exploring various aspects of our world and society, it is only fitting that we delve into the future and the potential outcomes that lie before us. The world is constantly evolving, and in this chapter, we will attempt to analyze the trajectory of our society, technological advancements, environmental sustainability, and the human experience.

1. Technological Advancements:

The exponential growth of technology over the past century has completely revolutionized the way we live, work, and interact. It is evident that this rapid pace of innovation will continue to shape our future profoundly. From artificial intelligence and automation to breakthroughs in biotechnology and clean energy, technological advancements are set to transform our lives in unimaginable ways.

The integration of AI into various sectors will not only enhance productivity but also create new job opportunities and redefine existing roles. Machine learning and data-driven insights will revolutionize healthcare, diagnostics, and treatment, leading to more accurate and personalized therapies. Automation will augment human capabilities and streamline repetitive tasks, allowing us to focus more on creative problem-solving and innovation.

2. Environmental Sustainability:

The looming threat of climate change and dwindling natural resources necessitates prompt action and strategic planning for a sustainable future. Renewable energy sources like solar, wind, and hydroelectric power are gaining significant investment and will gradually replace traditional energy sources. The advancement of battery technologies will further enhance the efficacy of renewable energy systems and pave the way for cleaner transportation alternatives.

Efforts to reduce carbon emissions and combat environmental degradation will be bolstered by the widespread adoption of green practices and the implementation of stringent environmental policies. Innovations in waste management and recycling will take center stage, enabling us to achieve circular economies that minimize waste and maximize resource utilization.

3. Human Experience:

As technology continues to shape our world, it is crucial to assess its impact on the human experience. The integration of virtual and augmented reality into everyday life will have far-reaching effects on entertainment, education, and even interpersonal relationships. Remote work and telecommuting will become more prevalent, offering greater flexibility and work-life balance.

However, it is essential that we strike a balance between the benefits of technological progress and preserving our core human values. The rise in automation calls for a renewed focus on re-skilling and continuous learning to adapt to the evolving employment landscape. Issues surrounding privacy, data security, and ethical considerations related to AI will become critical discussion points, necessitating robust frameworks and regulations.

4. Global Cooperation:

The challenges we face in the future, be it climate change, pandemics, or socioeconomic inequality, will require unprecedented levels of global cooperation. Collaboration among nations, organizations, and individuals will play a pivotal role in finding solutions to these complex problems. International agreements and frameworks centered around sustainability, healthcare, and poverty eradication will be critical for fostering a more unified and equitable world.

THE FUTURE OF OUR WORLD is full of possibilities and opportunities for growth and transformation. Technological advancements hold immense promise, but it is crucial that we wield them responsibly and ethically. The pursuit of environmental sustainability is no longer a choice but a necessity for the preservation of our planet. As we move forward, it is our collective responsibility to shape the future we want to see – a future that is inclusive, sustainable, and prosperous for all.

- Exploration of potential breakthroughs and advancements in climate solutions

Exploration of potential breakthroughs and advancements in climate solutions has become critically significant in our modern world. Climate change is one of the greatest challenges facing humanity, with the potential to greatly impact our ecosystems, economies, and overall quality of life.

Addressing climate change requires a combination of mitigation efforts (reducing greenhouse gas emissions) and adaptation strategies (adjusting to the impacts already occurring). While we have made some progress, the urgency of the climate crisis demands even greater breakthroughs and advancements in finding effective solutions.

One promising breakthrough lies in renewable energy technologies. The development of solar energy, wind power, and hydropower has advanced exponentially in recent years. The efficiency of solar panels has improved significantly, while the costs have drastically decreased. Similarly, wind turbines have become more efficient and reliable, making wind power a viable alternative to fossil fuels. Advancement in these technologies could dramatically reduce our reliance on carbon-intensive energy sources.

In addition, advancements in battery storage technology hold potential for revolutionizing the power sector. Despite the intermittent nature of solar and wind energy, efficient and cost-effective batteries can store excess energy for use during periods of low renewable generation. This discovery would eliminate the dependence on fossil fuels, allowing for a more stable and sustainable energy grid.

Another promising avenue of exploration lies in carbon capture and storage (CCS) technologies. CCS aims to capture carbon dioxide emissions produced mainly by power plants and industrial processes and store it underground permanently. The development of more efficient and economically viable CCS technologies can contribute significantly to reducing $CO2$ emissions.

Additionally, advancements in direct air capture technologies could allow us to capture CO2 already present in the atmosphere.

Furthermore, advancements in agricultural practices have the potential to play a substantial role in climate solutions. Improved soil management techniques, such as regenerative agriculture and agroforestry, can sequester carbon in agricultural soils and promote sustainable farming practices. These practices not only reduce greenhouse gas emissions but also improve soil health and increase resilience to climate change impacts.

Breakthroughs in climate-friendly transportation can also have a profound impact. The transition from internal combustion engines to electric vehicles (EVs) is already underway, but challenges remain concerning battery technology, charging infrastructure, and cost-efficiency. Advancements in these areas could accelerate the adoption of EVs and significantly reduce emissions from the transportation sector.

Additionally, investing in research and development of sustainable materials and technologies is essential. Advancements in alternative materials, such as bio-based plastics and construction materials, can greatly reduce the carbon footprint of various industries. Wood-based products as a substitute for energy-intensive materials like steel and concrete can also play a significant role in reducing emissions.

AI technology also presents potential breakthroughs in modeling and monitoring climate change. Advanced modeling techniques can help predict future climate scenarios accurately. Moreover, AI algorithms can aid in monitoring deforestation, illegal fishing, and other environmental challenges more efficiently.

While significant progress has been made in exploring these potential breakthroughs and advancements, more substantial investments in research and development are needed. Governments, international organizations, and the private sector must collaborate to accelerate the implementation of these solutions. Moreover, policies that incentivize innovation and support clean technologies can further drive breakthroughs in climate solutions.

Ultimately, the exploration of potential breakthroughs and advancements in climate solutions offers hope in tackling the urgent global climate crisis. With a concerted effort from governments, businesses, and society as a whole, we can strive towards a sustainable future and ensure the health and wellbeing of our planet for generations to come.

135

- Analysis of emerging technologies and their role in combatting global warming

Emerging technologies have a crucial role to play in combatting global warming. As our planet grapples with the devastating impacts of climate change, from rising temperatures to extreme weather events, it is clear that bold and innovative solutions are needed. In this analysis, we will examine some of the cutting-edge technologies that are shaping the fight against global warming and how they can mitigate its effects.

One of the promising technologies on the horizon is carbon capture, utilization, and storage (CCUS). This process involves capturing carbon dioxide (CO_2) emissions from power plants, factories, or even directly from the atmosphere, and then storing or using them in an environmentally friendly way. By preventing CO_2 from entering the atmosphere or repurposing it for industries such as cement manufacturing, this technology has the potential to significantly reduce greenhouse gas emissions.

Another crucial area of emerging technology is renewable energy generation. As nations strive to transition away from fossil fuels, technologies such as solar and wind power are becoming increasingly prevalent. Photovoltaics, for example, have experienced substantial advancements, with higher conversion efficiencies and lower production costs. By tapping into renewable sources of energy, countries can reduce their reliance on fossil fuels, lower emissions, and promote a more sustainable energy future.

Furthermore, advancements in energy storage technologies are essential for the widespread adoption of renewable energy sources. Batteries, for instance, are instrumental in storing excess energy generated by solar or wind systems for use during periods of low generation. Improving the efficiency and scalability of energy storage systems can help overcome the intermittent nature of renewable energy, making them more reliable and viable alternatives to fossil fuel-powered grids.

The transportation sector also plays a significant role in global warming, accounting for a substantial portion of greenhouse gas emissions. However, emerging technologies such as electric vehicles (EVs) are promising for reducing carbon footprints. With advancements in battery technology and charging infrastructure, EVs are becoming more affordable and widespread globally. Additionally, alternative fuels like hydrogen, biofuels, and ammonia are being explored as potential replacements for carbon-intensive gasoline or diesel.

Artificial intelligence (AI) also has the potential to be a game-changer in combatting global warming. AI-powered algorithms can optimize energy consumption, predict weather patterns, and enable efficient resource management. For example, intelligent grid systems can adjust the distribution of electricity based on real-time data and demand, reducing waste and minimizing emissions. AI-driven climate models can also provide more accurate forecasts and help policymakers make informed decisions to mitigate and adapt to climate change.

Although not entirely new, smart buildings are another emerging technology that holds promise in the battle against global warming. From energy-efficient designs to connected systems that optimize energy usage, smart buildings can considerably reduce greenhouse gas emissions. Conserving energy through smart lighting, automated heating and cooling systems, as well as monitoring occupancy to adjust energy consumption, are some of the key features. As the world continues to urbanize, smart buildings can contribute significantly to more sustainable cities.

The analysis of emerging technologies also cannot ignore the potential from advancements in agriculture and food production. Technologies such as vertical farming, precision agriculture, and gene editing can help address emissions generated by current agricultural practices. Vertical farms, for instance, use IoT-enabled automation and LED lighting to grow crops indoors, with significantly less water and land consumption compared to traditional farming methods. Precision agriculture leverages data and sensors to optimize water and fertilizer usage, minimizing waste. Gene editing holds the potential to improve crop resilience, increasing yields even under harsh climate conditions while reducing agricultural inputs.

In conclusion, emerging technologies hold great potential in combatting global warming. From carbon capture and renewable energy to electric vehicles, AI systems, smart buildings, and innovative agricultural practices, these technologies can collectively make a significant impact. As nations and industries collaborate and invest in these advancements, harnessing the power of innovation is essential for mitigating the effects of global warming and ensuring a more sustainable and habitable planet for future generations.

- Examination of potential scenarios and outcomes based on the actions taken

An examination of potential scenarios and outcomes based on the actions taken brings forth a plethora of opportunities for exploration and analysis. By delving deep into the specifics, we can better understand the consequences and implications of various choices made within a given context.

One potential scenario that can be explored is in the field of healthcare. When policymakers make decisions regarding healthcare reform, they must evaluate the potential outcomes of different approaches. For instance, in a hypothetical situation where a government decides to introduce universal healthcare, numerous factors need to be considered. These may include the impact on the national budget, public sentiment towards the change, and the level of access and quality of care provided to citizens.

In examining potential outcomes, one scenario could envision a positive impact on public health. Under universal healthcare, individuals would have increased access to medical services, preventive care, and screenings. This may result in earlier detection and treatment of diseases, leading to improved overall health outcomes for the population. Additionally, with a more significant focus on preventive measures, the burden to the healthcare system could potentially be reduced in the long run.

However, exploring potential scenarios also entails considering the drawbacks and challenges. For instance, in the case of universal healthcare, there might be potential financial strain on the government's budget. Funding such a comprehensive system could require significant tax increases or allocation of existing funds from other sectors, leading to opposition among some segments of the population. Additionally, the increased demand for medical services may strain health facilities, potentially resulting in longer wait times for appointments and procedures.

Another exploratory scenario could be the effects of implementing specific environmental policies. Actions taken to combat climate change, such as stricter regulations on emissions or investments in renewable energy sources, can have wide-ranging outcomes. A potential positive outcome might be a reduced carbon footprint, leading to cleaner air quality, an improved natural environment, and a minimized impact on climate change. Moreover, such actions could spur innovation and foster the growth of renewable energy industries, creating job opportunities and boosting the economy.

Conversely, the potential challenges and negative outcomes of such policies might include short-term economic disruptions. Industries reliant on fossil fuels may suffer as they adapt to new regulations or face increased competition from renewable energy sources. Adverse effects on certain sectors might emerge, requiring intervention to ensure a just transition and mitigate any adverse impacts on workers. Balancing economic concerns, environmental goals, and social equity is paramount in determining the most effective course of action.

These are just two examples of potential scenarios and outcomes resulting from specific actions. Examining these scenarios and their potential consequences allows policymakers, researchers, and stakeholders to make informed decisions based on a more comprehensive understanding of the situation at hand. Carefully analyzing both positive and negative outcomes enables us to anticipate challenges, maximize benefits, and develop holistic approaches that balance competing priorities.

Chapter 10: Conclusion

- Reiteration of the urgent need for immediate action to combat global warming

Global warming is a phenomenon that has reached alarming levels in recent years. It is imperative for us to understand the urgent need for immediate action to combat this issue before the consequences become irreversible.

Firstly, global warming is primarily caused by the excessive release of greenhouse gases into the atmosphere, mainly due to human activities such as burning fossil fuels and deforestation. These gases, including carbon dioxide and methane, create a greenhouse effect, trapping heat and causing the Earth's temperature to rise exponentially.

The implications of global warming are vast and catastrophic. Rising global temperatures lead to the melting of polar ice caps, causing a rise in sea levels. This, in turn, leads to more frequent and severe coastal flooding, jeopardizing low-lying areas and millions of people who reside in them. Additionally, the health impacts of global warming are severe, with increasingly frequent heatwaves leading to heat-related illnesses and deaths.

Moreover, the implications for our ecosystems are dire. The increasingly warmer temperatures disrupt delicate ecological balances, causing the extinction of numerous animal and plant species. The Great Barrier Reef, for example, has suffered extensive bleaching and is under threat of complete collapse if temperatures continue to rise.

Furthermore, global warming poses serious threats to agricultural productivity. Changes in rainfall patterns and prolonged droughts disrupt crop growth, leading to food scarcity and potential famine in many regions. This can exacerbate existing problems like poverty and political instability.

The urgency to combat global warming cannot be overstated. Experts warn that if we do not act immediately to curb our greenhouse gas emissions, we will reach a tipping point where the effects become irreversible. It is essential to transition to cleaner and renewable energy sources, such as solar and wind power, and reduce our dependence on fossil fuels.

Additionally, governments and individuals alike must take responsibility for their carbon footprint. This can be achieved through energy-efficient practices, adopting sustainable transportation options, and actively engaging in reforestation efforts. Political leaders must also prioritize climate action, forging international agreements to limit emissions and holding nations accountable for their commitments.

Education and awareness are crucial components of the fight against global warming. People must understand the gravity of the situation and the individual and collective actions needed to mitigate its effects. Governments and organizations should invest in campaigns that spread awareness and inspire citizens to take immediate action.

In conclusion, the urgent need for immediate action to combat global warming cannot be emphasized enough. The consequences of inaction are severe and wide-ranging, affecting not only our environment but our health, economies, and overall quality of life. It is our responsibility to act now, as individuals, communities, and nations, to reduce greenhouse gas emissions, adapt to the changing climate, and protect the Earth for future generations.

- Inspiration for readers to actively participate in the fight against global warming

In today's rapidly changing world, one of the biggest challenges our planet faces is global warming. The rise in greenhouse gas emissions, primarily caused by human activities, is leading to drastic changes in our climate system with far-reaching consequences. From extreme weather events to rising sea levels, the effects of global warming are being felt everywhere. However, amidst these grave circumstances, there is still hope. Every individual can contribute to the fight against global warming and help create a sustainable future for our planet.

One of the first steps in inspiring people to actively participate in this fight is by educating them about the importance of global warming and its implications. People need to understand that global warming is not just an abstract concept, but a real threat that affects their daily lives. Sharing and disseminating information about climate change, its causes, and its impacts can help raise awareness and inspire action.

Education alone is not enough; people also need to feel inspired and motivated to take action against global warming. Creating a sense of urgency is crucial in igniting this inspiration. Understanding that the choices we make today will shape the world for future generations can be a powerful motivator. Through compelling stories and examples, we can showcase the direct and indirect consequences of global warming, fueling individuals with a desire to make a difference.

Another way to inspire active participation is by highlighting success stories and showcasing the impact of collective action. When people see tangible results, they are more likely to believe in their own potential to effect change. Sharing stories of communities transitioning to renewable energy sources or individuals adopting sustainable lifestyles can give readers a sense of empowerment and encourage them to start their own journey in combating global warming.

Engaging readers on a personal level is also crucial. Climate change can sometimes feel overwhelming and distant, but by breaking it down into simple, actionable steps, we can empower individuals to make a difference in their own lives. Providing practical tips and suggestions on reducing carbon footprints, such as composting, using energy-efficient appliances, or opting for public transportation, can inspire readers to take small but impactful actions.

Furthermore, creating platforms for individuals to connect and collaborate with like-minded individuals can foster a sense of community and support. By joining hands, people can pool their resources, expertise, and ideas, amplifying their collective impact and creating a strong network of individuals committed to fighting global warming.

Lastly, it is essential to emphasize the role of individuals not only as consumers but also as responsible citizens. Encouraging readers to engage in advocacy for sustainable policies and supporting organizations working towards combating climate change can provide a channel for their passion and inspire them to make a difference at a higher level.

In conclusion, inspiring readers to actively participate in the fight against global warming requires education, motivation, engagement, and empowerment. Providing them with meaningful information, showcasing the impact of collective action, and offering practical steps to reduce carbon footprints can help readers feel inspired, motivated, and engaged. By highlighting success stories, fostering community, and emphasizing civic responsibility, we can encourage readers to become agents of change, dedicated to creating a sustainable and habitable planet for generations to come.